A Guide to Grammar and Usage for Psychology and Related Fields

John Eric Bellquist

1993

LAWRENCE ERLBAUM ASSOCIATES, PUBLISHERS

Hillsdale, New Jersey   Hove and London

Lawrence Erlbaum Associates, Inc., Publishers
365 Broadway
Hillsdale, New Jersey 07642

Library of Congress Cataloging-in-Publication Data
Bellquist, John Eric
    A guide to grammar and usage for psychology and related fields / John Eric Bellquist
        p. cm.
    ISBN 0-8058-1394-2.—ISBN 0-8058-1353-5 (pbk.)
    1. Psychology—Authorship. Psychology, Experimental—Authorship 3. Science—Authorship 4. Authorship—Style manuals. 5. English language—Grammar—1950—Handbooks, manuals, etc.
    I. Title.
BF76.8.B44 1993
808'.06615—dc20   92-39627
                                                                        CIP

Books published by Lawrence Erlbaum Associates are printed on acid-free paper, and their bindings are chosen for strength and durability.

Printed in the United States of America
10 9 8 7 6 5 4 3 2 1

List of Entries*

Endnotes and a selected bibliography appear at the end of this volume.

A

a, an,   1
abbreviations, Latin,   1
abbreviations of measurement,   3
abbreviations, statistical,   5
abbreviations of terms,   7
above,   14
additional, additionally,   15
adverbs versus adjectives,   17
adverbs, conjunctive,   19
adverbs, hyphenation of,   19
adverbs, placement of,   19
age, aged,   23
agreement,   23
among,   26
and,   26
ANOVA,   26
apostrophes,   27
as,   29
as shown,   30
as to,   30
avoid,   30

B

based on, on the basis of,   31
be,   32
because,   32
between,   33
between group, within group; between-group, within-group,   34
between subject[s], within subjects; between-subject[s], within-subjects,   35

both, adjective,   35
both…and,   36
brain,   37
but,   38

C

cannot, can't,   39
cf.,   39
collinear,   39
colons,   39
commas,   41
  commas with appositives,   41
  commas and coordination: compound sentences and compound verbs or predicates,   42
  commas with *for example* or *that is,*   45
  commas with nonrestrictive, as opposed to restrictive, modifiers,   46
  commas with opening phrases,   47
  comma placement and meaning,   48
  commas in series,   48
  commas between subjects and verbs,   49
  commas and subordination: adverbial clauses,   50
  commas with transitional words,   50
comparison,   51
  comparisons with *similar to, the same as,* etc.,   52
  the comparative with *than,*   58
  comparisons with the verb *to compare,*   61
compose, comprise,   61
comprise,   63

---

*Italics indicate letters, words, or phrases used as linguistic examples.

condition, conditioned,   63
consistent with,   63
coordination,   64

D

dashes,   68
degrees of freedom,   69
discrimination by,   70
do,   70
dosage, dose,   70
due to,   70

E

each,   72
each vs. *a, an,* or *the,*   72
easily vs. *easy to,*   73
effects and interactions,   73
either...or...,   74
e.g.,   75
example,   76
exclamation marks,   76
experiment, experiments,   76
experiments, personification of,   77

F

find, found,   78
findings by, from, in, and *of,*   78
following,   78
for example,   79
further vs. *furthermore,*   80

G

generality, generalize,   81
gerunds,   83
gestalt, Gestalt,   83

H

hands-on,   83
having,   84
high-frequency, low-frequency,   84
hippocampal,   85
hyphenated terms,   85
  hyphenated adjectives,   85
  hyphenated versus nonhyphenated
    nouns and noun phrases,   90
  hyphenation of prefixes,   92

I

identical to,   93
i.e.,   93

if...then,   93
imagery,   96
impact,   97
imperatives or infinitives as modifi-
    ers,   97
importantly,   99
increase, increase with,   100
independent,   102
-ing words,   102
in order to,   106
interactions,   106
interesting to note,   106
involve,   107

J, L

jargon,   107
latter, the,   108
left-handed,   108
lists in text,   108
long-term,   108
lowercase, uppercase,   108
-ly,   108

M

maintain,   108
manuscripts, preparation of,   109
meaning,   112
measurement, units of,   114
memory for,   114
method, methodology,   114
mixed constructions,   115
mode, modality,   118
modification,   119

N

necessary,   126
neither...nor...,   126
not...or...,   126
nouns and nominalization,   127

O

on,   131
on [the] average,   131
one-way, two-way,   131
optionally,   131

P, Q

parallelism,   132
passive voice,   135

participles, present,   138
perception by,   139
periods,   139
personification,   140
pre-,   142
predication, statement,   143
prior to,   145
problematic,   146
pronouns,   146
   pronoun reference or anaphora,   146
   pronouns and "gender,"   148
punctuation,   150
purpose,   150
purpose, construction of,   152
questions and question marks,   154

R

reaction time,   154
reference,   155
refers to,   155
repeated measures,   156
repetition,   156
required,   157
response time, response times,   158
right-handed,   158
run (verb and noun),   158

S

same as, the,   158
same–different,   158
same, the, vs. *this same,*   159
see (vs. *cf.* or *e.g.*),   159
semicolons,   160
   semicolons with   coordinated
      clauses,   160
   semicolons with lists,   161
similar to,   162
since,   162
so that, such that,   162
spelling,   163

stand-alone,   165
statement,   165
stimulus–response language,   165
study, studies,   167
style,   167
subjects,   170
subjunctive,   171
submit,   171
such that,   172
support, supportive,   172

T

tense,   173
tense, present continuous,   176
terms, consistency of,   176
that, conjunction,   177
that vs. *which,*   178
the,   178
there is, there are,   180
this latter, the latter,   180
to, in order,   180
to, lexical decisions to, ERPs to, etc.,   181
transitional words and phrases,   181

U, V

uppercase,   183
use, using,   183
versus,   185
via,   185
viz.,   186

W

where,   186
which,   187
while,   190
within group(s),   190
within subjects,   190
wordiness,   190

Preface

This style manual is intended, first, for experimental psychologists and students in the field of experimental psychology, as a means of assistance in the preparation of papers for presentation or publication, or for submission as course work. But because experimental psychologists are scientists and experimental psychology is a science, I hope that scientists and students of science in other fields will find some helpful information here, too. Most publications in experimental psychology, apart from reviews of the present state of knowledge in given fields of research or the occasional book review, consist of the discussion of experiments, and because experimental research is the fundamental means of scientific work, it is possible that anyone engaged in scientific experimentation and in writing about it may find in these pages some profitable advice.

This is not a complete publication manual, or a book on writing the scientific psychology paper, both of which are already available.* It is rather a commentary on points of grammatical usage and style that seem, from an editor's point of view, to represent concerns or issues that repeatedly arise when authors write about experimentation in psychology. To my knowledge, no other publication adequately provides such information. Much of the grammatical and stylistic advice that has been published to aid scientific writ-

*Publication Manual of the American Psychological Association (3rd ed., rev.). (1984). Washington, DC: American Psychological Association. R.J. Sternberg, *Writing the Psychology Paper* (1977). Woodbury, NY: Barron's Educational Series.

ers, for example, reads as if it has been written by English teachers who have in mind writers who do not publish in scientific fields, or by scientific writers who think that their peers merely need the information that is already available in the countless handbooks on grammar and style for student writers in English classes. But such traditional handbooks seldom offer the particular sorts of commentary that the scientific writer needs.

My own background also includes that of the English teacher. Probably this alone would never have led me to write a handbook of the present sort. But for the past 4 years, I have been employed at the publications and business office of the Psychonomic Society, a professional organization of experimental psychologists that may perhaps be most easily defined as a smaller, more specialized version of the American Psychological Association, with a more restricted membership. During that time I have been involved in the copy editing, and also in the editorial production, of between 200 and 300 articles per year published in the journals *Animal Learning & Behavior; Behavior Research Methods, Instruments, & Computers;* the *Bulletin of the Psychonomic Society; Memory & Cognition; Perception & Psychophysics;* and *Psychobiology.* This activity has made me well acquainted with the peculiar stylistic and grammatical graces and weaknesses of writers in experimental psychology and the many scientific fields that are allied with it—characteristics of style that often only editors are permitted to witness, before an author's writing is remolded into suitably publishable shape.

This experience has also made me well aware of the attitudes of scientific writers toward scientific writing and toward editing and editors—a relationship that is for the most part amicable or congenial, but that at times can turn surprisingly hostile. This is of course nothing new—even in the humanities, no less a scholar than Jacques Barzun has objected to the apparent ignorance or cavalier disregard of copy editors for the manuscripts that they edit. In the case of scientific writing, this possibility can be all the worse, because copy editors are often relatively unskilled in the scientific writer's particular field of expertise. Yet it is the copy editor's job to attend to form and style, whereas the scientific writer will always focus more on content. The guidelines that follow represent my own opinions, although they have been shaped very much through discussion with writers and with other editors. Some readers may think that I am at times somewhat opinionated. If so, I am not different from most authors of handbooks on style and usage. Such handbooks must make recommendations; they cannot merely offer empirical descriptions of the language in its present state. Ideally, they should reflect the opinions of the best writers of the language. If this means risking the accusation of being "prescriptive," there is nothing wrong with that. Most people who look up words in dictionaries are looking for the "right" way to use them. But I am much less concerned that scientific writers should follow my guidelines than I am hopeful that my recommendations will at least lead them to think still more carefully about their use of English than they already do. Once they have done that, if they make choices other than those that I recommend, at least their choices will be "informed," and they will be able to defend their choices if necessary.

Such a set of guidelines could be presented in various forms, but here it has seemed most useful to arrange the material alphabetically, with as much cross-referencing as possible. Writers who use this guide will most likely be looking up specific points, rather than desiring to read chapters. The choice of topics has not been governed by my own interests about the English language nearly as much as it has resulted from the writing of scientists in the field. If, for example, the entry on comparison or on modification is much longer than that on agreement, this is because, on the basis of my experience as an editor, semantic problems in the written discussion of statistical comparisons or in the construction of verbal modifications are demonstrably more prevalent than errors of grammatical number in the scientific writing of experimental psychologists. If any particular point of grammar seems to be missing, that is because it does not appear to be a difficult issue for the authors whom I am accustomed to edit. If I sometimes seem inclined to give a rather large number of examples, I do so because I think that they are illustrative and that the writer who is willing to study them well will benefit from doing so. Every entry and every example has been dictated by the current practice of scientific writers themselves. Many of the examples are direct quotes. None, unless it is appended with a footnote, is taken verbatim from any publication, but all are at least loosely based on actual written constructions that I have frequently encountered.

ACKNOWLEDGMENTS

I should not have been able to write this guide without the implicit support of the Psychonomic Society's business and publications office. There I have been able to study a wide range of journals, to gather many written examples, and to discuss the fine points of editing regularly with other members of the editorial staff. I especially wish to thank Ellen Woodard, the executive director, and Anne Dossett, the managing editor, for giving me the opportunity to write this book. I should also like to thank the other editors—Calvin Cahan, Diane Hall, and Michael Slattery—with whom I have discussed many of the topics in this book almost daily; as is always true among editors, our discussions have sometimes been vigorous, but they have always proved fruitful. To all of these colleagues I am indebted for their suggesting several of the examples that follow, for reading portions of the manuscript, and for offering me their very helpful advice.

John Eric Bellquist

A

a, an. *A* and *an* are the two forms of the indefinite article in English. *A* is used before words that begin with consonants: *a lexical decision task. An* is used before words that begin with vowels: *an effect.* When a word begins with the voiced "h" in English, the word is construed as beginning with a consonant: *a hit, a high-frequency tone.* When a word begins with a silent "h," however, the word is construed as if it begins with a vowel: *an honor, an honest person.* (This silent "h" is a trace of the original pronunciation in French, where the initial "h" is always silent: *honneur, honnête.*) Despite what one occasionally sees in print or hears on the radio, the expression *a history* is therefore correct; the hypercorrected form *an history* is wrong. Another word that sometimes erroneously attracts *an* is *hypothesis,* which comes from Greek; but in both Greek and English, the initial "h" in this word is voiced: *a hypothesis.*

abbreviations, Latin. The discussion of scientific experiments includes the *specification* of problems, procedures, results, and their implications; it also includes the *comparison* of present effects or results, as well as of present research and its historical antecedents. The following abbreviations of Latin terms are often used to express such relationships.

Comparison
cf.   *confer,* compare
vs.   *versus,* against

Specification
e.g.   *exempli gratia,* for example
etc.   *et cetera,* and so forth (literally: and other things)
i.e.   *id est,* that is
viz.   *videlicet,* namely

These abbreviations do not need to be italicized to signify their foreign origin; they have long been English expressions in their own right. Note, too, that the punctuation does not necessarily reflect whether the respective abbreviation stands for one or two words in the Latin. *Et cetera* is two words, but it takes one period in its abbreviated form. It is therefore best to learn the conventional punctuation for each case separately.

The APA manual counsels that one use the preceding abbreviations within parentheses only; outside parentheses, they are to be spelled out, and their appropriate English counterparts should be used whenever common ones are available. Thus, for *et cetera,* one might use *and so forth* or *and so on;* and for *id est,* one should use *that is;* but *versus* has itself become an ordinary English word, so no counterpart for it is necessary.

Of the many other Latin abbreviations that may at times be useful, special attention should be paid to *et al.* (*et alii,* and others) and *ad lib* (*ad libitum,* in accordance with desire). *Et al.* is ordinarily used in APA style for citations of texts by three or more authors after their first mention, and for citations of texts by six or more authors always. It is never italicized or spelled out, and never translated. Note that *al.* is followed by a period. *Ad lib* is hyphenated when it is used as an adjective before the noun; otherwise it is not: *ad-lib feeding,* but *the rats were fed ad lib. Ad lib,* unlike *et al.,* does not take the period, even though logic would suggest that it should.

For additional comments, especially with respect to semantic problems sometimes associated with the use of such abbreviations, see CF., E.G., I.E., SEE, VIZ., and VERSUS.

abbreviations of measurement. In general, one should follow the APA manual in abbreviating units of measurement; when this does not suffice, one should follow the guidelines provided by professional societies or organizations in other fields, and particularly those found in the publication manual of the American Institute of Physics. Yet there will always be some units of measurement that one cannot seem to find anywhere, and journals do differ: The journals of the Psychonomic Society, for example, do not follow the APA's guidelines in all respects. In fact, anyone who reads much in the field of experimental psychology will discover variation even within single journals, usually owing to editors' having followed the practice of particular authors, but sometimes owing to editorial inconsistency. The APA's own journals are no exception to this observation.

Here is a brief selection of common abbreviations of measurement; those with asterisks should be defined within parentheses on first use:[1]

cd	candle(s), candela(s)
cm	centimeter(s)
cpd*	cycles per degree
cpm*	cycles per minute
cps*	cycles per second
deg, °	degree(s)
deg/s, deg/sec; °/s, °/sec	degree(s) per second (cf. dps)
dpi*	dot(s) per inch
dps*	degree(s) per second (cf. deg/s)

fc	foot-candle(s)
fL	foot-lambert(s)
ft	foot (feet)
g	gram(s)
hr, h	hour(s)
Hz	hertz
in.	inch(es); note the period
k	kilo-, except in kilobytes
K	kilobyte(s)
kc	kilocycle(s)
kg	kilogram(s)
kHz	kilohertz
kΩ	kilohm(s)
L	lambert(s)
m	meter(s)
M	molar concentration
MB	megabyte(s)
mg	milligram(s)
mHz	megahertz
min	minute(s) (time)
′	minute(s) (plane angle)
mm	millimeter(s)
ms, msec	millisecond(s)
μs, μsec	microsecond(s)
N	newton(s)
Ω	ohm(s)
rpm	revolution(s) per minute
s, sec	second(s) (time)
″	second(s) (plane angle)
V	volt(s)
W	watt(s)

Note that of these abbreviations, only the one for *inches* takes the period, to avoid confusion with the word *in: The circles were 2 in. in diameter.*

As for the hyphenation of such abbreviations, consider the following examples (again, practice will sometimes vary):

a 5-s interval (a 5-sec interval)
an interval of 5 s (an interval of 5 sec)

a 3-min test
a test 3 min long

a 1- to 5-s interval (a 1- to 5-sec interval)

2-, 5-, and 10-s exposures (2-, 5-, and 10-sec exposures)

a 25-cm-diam platter
a platter 25 cm in diameter

a 12:12-hr light:dark cycle (a 12:12-h light:dark cycle)

5 × 7 in. cards
a 25 × 25 cm box

an interval of 1–5 days
from 1 to 5 days

a temperature of 22–24° C
temperature from 22° to 24° C

Note that in general, the numeral and the abbreviation take the hyphen when they act together as a compound adjective before the noun, as in the first six examples just given; but when the adjectival construction becomes too complex, as in the example *5 × 7 in. cards, a 25 × 25 cm box,* the hyphen is omitted.[2]

abbreviations, statistical. Among the many abbreviations of statistical or mathematical terms, the following are common:

α alpha: probability of Type I error
β beta: probability of Type II error

χ^2	chi-square
d'	d prime
df, df	degrees of freedom
F	denotes the *F* test or analysis of variance
f	denotes functions
hsd, HSD	honestly significant difference
jnd, JND	just noticeable difference
lsd, LSD	least significant difference
M	mean
MS_e	mean square error
N	total number
n	number in a portion of the total
n.s.	not significant
p	probability
r	Pearson product-moment correlation coefficient
Σ	sigma: summation of
SD	standard deviation
SE	standard error
SEM	standard error of the mean
SS	sum of squares
t	denotes Student's *t* test
T	denotes the Wilcoxon *T* test
τ	tau: Kendall rank correlation coefficient
U	denotes the Mann-Whitney *U* test

Note that Greek letters do not have an italic form, so they should never be underlined in a manuscript. Without numerical values, they may be spelled out (alpha, beta, etc.); with numerical values, they should remain as Greek letters. Hence one may write of *chi-square*, but one would write that χ^2 (4, $N = 80$) = 9.76. As for certain of these abbreviations, usage seems to vary. Some authors, editors, or publishers prefer the italic *df*; others prefer the roman df. Some writers prefer the uppercase HSD, JND, and LSD over the lowercase hsd, jnd, and lsd; still others would use italics for either of these sets of forms. Traditionally, however, jnd seems to be most common. Whichever choice one makes, one should be consistent within a given paper; to write of jnd and HSD in the same context can be confusing.

abbreviations of terms. Abbreviations of terms pervade the writing of experimental psychologists. Sometimes the use of such abbreviations may seem questionable, for they can be used to suggest that reality is quantifiable even when it is not, or they can permit an artificial schematization of experience when empirical observation does not warrant it. A writer should never invent abbreviations merely to organize the obvious; in a study of young children's preferences for playing with various objects, for example, it would be absurd to label a toy truck T, a toy car C, a doll D, and so on. Moreover, to resort mechanically to abbreviations of terms sometimes lends a needlessly official imprimatur, with which a writer can implicitly claim to be included, regardless of scientific merit, among the restricted group of people who are privy to the esoteric discourse of experimental psychology. Abbreviations of terms thus confer on the scientific writer what sociolinguists call *covert prestige.*

In support of abbreviations of terms, however, it must be argued that when used well they save space, and that when abbreviations stand for particularly long and unwieldy locutions, they contribute to a precision and an economy of style. Yet this does not mean that one may make up abbreviations for terms at will and utilize them with abandon. One should be careful not to use many such abbreviations within a single paper, and one should remember that they often cause clutter that obscures meaning, whether in paragraphs or even in sentences:

> *Experiments 1 and 2 show that SOA provides an adequate parameter for the WWE and that the range of speeds reported here for AM lies comfortably with the range over which RM is seen.*[3]

Although it is true that the writers of the preceding sentence defined each of these abbreviations clearly in their paper, and that the first one (for stimulus onset asynchrony) is commonly understood, nonetheless the inclusion of four such abbreviations within a single sentence does not usually bode well for the reader's immediate understanding of what a writer is trying to say. Indeed, if every writer were to endeavor to use abbreviations this prolifically, the limits of the alphabet would quickly result in too few abbreviations standing for far too many things.

The following two lists illustrate the confusion or inconsistency that can arise from the abbreviation of terms:[4]

CR	contingent reinforcement
CR	critical range
CRF	consistent reinforcement
CRF	continuous reinforcement
D-R	drive reinforcement
DRH	differential reinforcement of high rates
DRL	differential reinforcement of low rates
DRO	differential reinforcement of other behavior
MULT	multiple schedule of reinforcement
N	nonreinforcement (cf. NR below)
NCR	noncontingent reinforcement
NR	no reinforcement
PRE	potential reinforcement effect
PREE	partial reinforcement extinction effect
PRF	partial reinforcement
PRF	potential reinforcement
RFT	reinforcement
S	short
S	stimulus
S	subject
ST	semitone

These examples show that the same letters may stand for diverse categories or concepts, even within the same field of research, and that nothing systematic is likely to be achieved through their use, if they are held to be equally valid. Here,

R, RF, and RFT all stand for *reinforcement,* but R also stands for *range;* P stands for both *partial* and *potential;* D means both *drive* and *differential.* When one keeps in mind the most common abbreviations—S for *stimulus,* R for *reaction* or *response,* and RT for *reaction time* or *response time*—the piling up of other similar forms leads to unnecessary complexity. These abbreviations have of course been taken from several papers; yet all of those in the first group come from papers on related topics, and it is also true that some writers seem inclined to use handfuls of equally confusing abbreviations within single paragraphs.

Therefore, the best policy regarding such abbreviations is to use them sparingly, and to do so only if they will demonstrably help the reader. Because certain terms are unwieldy when read repeatedly, abbreviations can make them much easier to assimilate: ANOVA for *analysis of variance* and ERP for *event-related brain potential* are good examples. But there is no need to multiply abbreviations beyond the dictates of common sense.

Among the most common abbreviations, S, R, S–R, CR, RT, and ANOVA seem to be universally accepted (for *stimulus, reaction* or *response, stimulus–response, conditioned response, reaction* or *response time,* and, again, *analysis of variance*); within certain specific fields of experimental psychology, others are also common (see the following list). The once frequent roman uppercase S for *subject* (Ss for *subjects*), on the other hand, has fallen into disuse, presumably because it sounds dehumanizing or because it can too easily become confused with S for *stimulus.* The APA manual recommends that abbreviations not yet included in the dictionary should be introduced in parentheses following their spelled out forms—*reaction times (RTs) were measured*—even if they are so common as to be understood by anyone at all familiar with experimental psychology. Although this rule may seem superfluous in the case of an acronym such as ANOVA, it should nonetheless be followed for consistency's sake.

Here are some guidelines for the use or the invention of abbreviations of terms:

1. Define all abbreviations germane to experimental psychology but not found in the dictionary. Thus there is no need to define cos for *cosine,* diam for *diameter,* or i.p. for *intraperitoneal,* but one should define ANOVA, CS, or RT. Do so the first time that the term to be abbreviated occurs, and use the abbreviation from then on throughout the text.

2. Be consistent. Do not employ both US and UCS for *unconditioned stimulus* in the same paper.

3. Let each letter stand for the beginning of a separate word as often as possible (ANOVA, however, is an excellent exception). It is simple to understand that R might stand for either *response* or *reaction* in the abbreviation RT for *reaction time,* if so explained; the abbreviation RFT for reinforcement, on the other hand, is unnecessarily complicated, because it makes the reader unsure whether the letters F or T, if used separately, would stand for words or parts of words. Probably the word *reinforcement* does not need an abbreviation at all, anyway.

4. Let each letter stand for only one form of the word to which it refers. Thus if RT means *reaction time,* RTs, with the plural "s," means *reaction times.* If CR is to mean *conditional response* rather than *conditioned response,* make this clear at the outset; do not mix the terms *conditioned* and *conditional* elsewhere within the paper, and do not let CR stand for both of them, even though they may be synonymous. Again, if H and V stand for the nouns or adjectives *horizontal* and *vertical* *(there were two axes: H and V),* do not use them in sentences in which the grammar and syntax would suggest that they mean *horizontally* and *vertically (the axis was oriented V or H).*

5. Let each letter stand not just for one form of a word, but for one word only. The following example may be instructive. When Crowder and Morton, writing in 1969, introduced their theory of "precategorical acoustic storage," they abbreviated it with the letters "PAS" throughout their

paper.[5] Careful attention to their use of this abbreviation will show that, in every instance, "PAS" could be translated back into the term *precategorical acoustic storage* without any trouble: "PAS bears important qualitative similarities to the comparable precategorical storage system in vision" (p. 365); "we shall first describe the PAS system and its properties" (p.365); "the consequences of PAS for immediate memory will be identified after the general system...is described in somewhat more detail" (p. 366); "the main feature of PAS is that it is capable of holding information sufficiently long enough to affect the immediate memory task" (p. 366); and so on. Subsequent writers who have chosen to agree or to argue with Crowder and Morton have attempted to borrow their terminology, but they have not always been consistent: Some speak of the precategorical acoustic *store* instead of *storage.* This presents no problem when a writer intends the term *store* instead of *storage* throughout his or her paper—although even then, one may wonder whether it is correct to attribute to Crowder and Morton a term that they did not in fact use—but if a writer goes as far as to use *store* and *storage* interchangeably in a paper, and if that writer then attempts to apply the abbreviation PAS to both of them, strange semantic incongruities will result. If PAS stands for *precategorical acoustic store,* it must be called *the PAS.* If, however, it means *precategorical acoustic storage,* it will be rendered as simply PAS. Neither the abbreviation PAS nor the phrase *the PAS* can correctly signify both *store* and *storage.* Unfortunately, many writers are insensitive to such subtleties; they apparently assume that because they mean the same thing as Crowder and Morton did, even though they have chosen to use the term *store* instead of *storage,* or to use the two terms interchangeably, their sentences about "PAS" are always correct. This assumption is faulty; it represents ungrammatical writing and lazy thought. In summary, an abbreviation can stand successfully for one and only one term within a given context. Likewise, if by RT one means *response time* rather than *reaction time,* one should be careful not to confuse the two.

6.   Try not to use more than two or at the most three abbreviations of terms in a single paragraph, particularly if they are unrelated (i.e., S, CS, R, and CR may fit well together within a fairly short space, but a like number of abbreviations referring to divergent categories, or of abbreviations less commonly used among other writers, cannot; see the earlier example with SOA, WWE, AM, and RM).

7.   When the abbreviation of a term is introduced, it should be given in a parenthesis immediately after the word(s) for which it stands. The abbreviation should never be located any earlier or later than that. Thus, the phrase *working (WM) and reference (RM) memory* makes no sense, because the abbreviations occur before the terms are given in full; *working memory (WM) and reference memory (RM)* makes sense, because each term is spelled out completely before each parenthesis, which follows the corresponding term at once.

8. Assume, unless you know otherwise, that the reader does not substitute the term while reading the abbreviation, but rather silently reads the letters. Therefore, it is correct to write *an RT of 30 sec,* but it is incorrect to write *a RT of 30 sec,* because the reader does not silently read *reaction time* for *RT.* Again, it is correct to write *a sodium chloride–sucrose mixture,* whereas *a NaCl–sucrose mixture* is incorrect; in the latter instance, one should instead refer to *an NaCl–sucrose mixture.* Although this principle may seem obvious, in the case of less common abbreviations, it sometimes is not. For an unusual instance in which the abbreviation is always construed as a word in itself, however, consider the following idiosyncratic and rather infelicitous computer term: *a SCSI port* ("a scuzzy port" or "a sexy port").

9.   The plural form of abbreviations takes the *-s:* as stated above, when one means *reaction times,* not *reaction time,* one should therefore write *RTs.*

The following brief list of abbreviations is admittedly

miscellaneous. It includes some of those that are most common among experimental psychologists. (See also ABBREVIATIONS OF MEASUREMENT.)

ac	alternating current
2AFC	two-alternative forced choice
a.m.	ante meridiem
ANOVA	analysis of variance
CR	conditioned response
CRT	cathode-ray tube
cos	cosine
CS	conditioned stimulus
CVC	consonant-vowel-consonant
D/A	digital/analog
dc	direct current
diam	diameter
d max	upper limit of spatial displacement
DMTS	delayed matching-to-sample
DOE	differential-outcomes effect
EP	evoked potential
ERP	event-related potential, event-related brain potential
$F0$	fundamental frequency
$F1$	first formant frequency
$F2$	second formant frequency
FA	false alarm
FFT	fast Fourier transform
FI	fixed interval
FR	fixed ratio
2IFC	two-interval forced choice
i.p.	intraperitoneal
IRI	interresponse interval
IRT	interresponse time
ISI	interstimulus interval
ITI	intertrial interval
i.v.	intravenous
LDT	lexical decision task

LED	light-emitting diode
lim	limit
ln	natural logarithm
log	logarithm
LTM	long-term memory
LVF	left visual field
max	maximum
min	minimum
MTS	matching-to-sample
n.s.	not significant
PE	percent error
p.m.	post meridiem
ROC	receiver-operating characteristic
RT	reaction time, response time
RVF	right visual field
s.c.	subcutaneous
SDT	signal-detection theory
sin	sine
SOA	stimulus onset asynchrony
S–O–R	stimulus–organism–response
S–R	stimulus–response
STM	short-term memory
UCS	unconditioned stimulus
US	unconditioned stimulus (cf. UCS above)
VF	visual field
VI	variable interval
VOT	voice onset time

above. *Above* is better off used as a preposition or an adverb, rather than an attributive adjective (*the above studies*) or an apparent noun (*see the above*). Although current usage and even historical example may permit one to write about *the above argument* with impunity, most writers who dislike jargon will still prefer *the argument above* or *the preceding argument*. Not only that, the use of *above* as an attributive adjective can sometimes be confusing:

*Ashcroft and Battaglia (1978) empirically tested the above counting
and direct-access/counting models, using verification tasks for simple addition problems.*[6]

In this example, it is at first hard to understand how *above* is
to be taken. Does it, one wonders at least momentarily, mean
a model somehow above counting, or a model previously
mentioned? The following version is better:

*Ashcroft and Battaglia (1978) empirically tested the counting and
direct-access/counting models mentioned above, by using verification tasks for simple addition problems.*

additional, additionally. *Additionally,* meaning *in addition,* is an adverb derived from the adjective *additional,* which
is in turn derived from the noun *addition.* Of these three
words, the adjective and especially the adverb are often,
although not always, dispensable. In the sentence *At the
suggestion of an anonymous reviewer, we performed an additional
experiment,* the adjective *additional* applies to the noun *experiment,* signifying that in addition to the original experiment
or experiments, the researchers have done one more, but the
writer could just as well have referred to *another experiment*
or *one more experiment* instead of *an additional experiment,*
either of which would be more direct and concise. Similarly,
additional research means *more research.* And the redundant
phrase *an additional fourth experiment* literally means that
there are two fourth experiments, which is impossible. The
adverb *additionally* is likewise often unnecessary or inappropriate, whether it modifies single verbs, adjectives, or other
adverbs. One does not *additionally run a fourth experiment;* one
simply runs *a fourth experiment.* A duration is not *additionally
long;* it is simply *longer.* One does not work *additionally hard;*
one works *harder.*

Scientific writers often use *additionally* to make transitions
from sentence to sentence, assuming that it can function after
the manner of *furthermore, however,* or *nevertheless* (see TRAN-
SITIONAL WORDS AND PHRASES). But one should remember that

outside scientific writing, this use of *additionally* rarely, if ever, occurs, and that even within scientific writing, it can create rhetorical dead weight:

> *Brigell and Uhlarik (1979) first reported that a 60-sec inspection of a contextual line produced length contrast in a subsequently judged test line. Additionally, Jordan and Uhlarik (1985) reported that this length aftereffect could be induced by only 5 sec of prior inspection of a contextual line.*[7]

In this quote, *additionally* is ambiguous, because it can mean either of two things. It can signify that the author is adding a second point in an ongoing argument, thereby stressing that not only Brigell and Uhlarik but also Jordan and Uhlarik found the aftereffect in question, or it can mean that Jordan and Uhlarik's findings were somehow in themselves additive with respect to those of Brigell and Uhlarik. This distinction is important: In the former instance, the term will be construed as representing the point of view of the author; in the latter, it must represent or imply the point of view of the researchers whose names are the subjects of the respective sentences. The confusion caused by this ambiguity results from the fact that *additionally* is not traditionally used as a conjunctive adverb of transition. Had the author written *furthermore,* one would know at once that the author's argument, rather than the sequence of the researchers' findings, was important. Yet even apart from this potential ambiguity, *additionally* is unnecessary in the passage. In the opening sentence, the author has set up a temporal sequence by using the word *first* to refer to Brigell and Uhlarik (1979); when the work of Jordan and Uhlarik (1985) is cited, the reader is already well prepared for it, and the use of *additionally* suggests that the writer is perhaps too immature to let the natural, chronological transition speak for itself. Rather than effect a fluent transition, *additionally* thus becomes an obstruction in the reader's path. *Additionally* is an awkward means of transition at best; the more graceful writer will avoid it and will use expressions such as *in addition, also, too,* or *later*—and sometimes nothing at all—instead.

adverbs versus adjectives. Before the 19th century, many English words functioned as both adjectives and adverbs. In the 17th and 18th centuries, it was thus acceptable to say *I am exceeding displeased*, rather than *I am exceedingly displeased*, or *the weather was terrible hot*, rather than *terribly hot*. Contemporary English too contains certain words that act as both adjectives and adverbs: *fast* (*a fast runner; she ran fast*), *hard* (*a hard task; he worked hard*), and *right* (*the right way; do it right*) are examples. Apart from such straightforward instances, however, which are derived from earlier inflected forms of these words, the mixing of adverbial and adjectival functions is not generally approved among educated speakers of English today. Note too that in the early set of instances just given, the adverbial adjective is always used as an intensifier, and that, in the three contemporary examples that follow, the two grammatical functions cannot be confused. In the phrases *a hard job* and *working hard*, the word *hard* has two different meanings, both of which are clear to anyone who speaks English.

The reason why the conflation of adverbs and adverbs is not usually approved in contemporary English is twofold. On the one hand, it reflects a deeply ingrained sociolinguistic etiquette, which brands anyone as illiterate who would say or write *he spoke cordial* (rather than *cordially*) *to her*, even though *he was cordial to her* is thought correct. On the other hand, it suggests the desire of grammarians and their followers for clarity. To distinguish *poor* from *poorly*, for example, prevents the ambiguity that might intrude into communication if *poor* were the only form of the word in use.

Nevertheless, among contemporary writers of scientific papers there is a tendency to let certain adjectives function as if they were adverbs, without regard to either of the aforementioned principles. The most common instance is the popular preference for substituting prepositional phrases introduced by the participial construction BASED ON for adverbial prepositional phrases introduced by ON THE BASIS OF; by definition, a participle is an adjective, not an adverb, and so the use of the one form to cover both grammatical functions often yields semantic confusion. Note that this is quite different from the use of the adjective as an adverbial intensifier, illustrated in the phrase *exceeding displeased,* that was common 250 years ago. The author who does not use BASED ON with care repeatedly runs the risk of being misunderstood.

Of single adjectival words that scientists often use as if they were adverbs, some of the most common are *independent, consistent, contingent,* and *similar,* although other instances abound. The following examples are typical: *the object was positioned collinear with the subject's eye and the target (the object was collinear with the subject's eye and the target; the object was positioned collinearly with the subject's eye and the target); this effect occurred independent of corticosterone level (this effect was independent of corticosterone level; this effect occurred independently of corticosterone level); consistent with the predictions of this model, there is evidence that…(consistent with the predictions of this model is the evidence that…; in agreement with the predictions of this model, there is evidence that…; There is evidence consistent with the predictions of this model. It is…); hippocampal activity increased, contingent on increases in ISI (hippocampal activity increased as ISI increased; increases in hippocampal activity were contingent on increases in ISI);* and so on. The variety among the corrected versions in parentheses suggests that a single adverbial use of the adjective has been allowed to substitute for a wide range of grammatical possibilities.

The distinction between adverbs and adjectives is thus ultimately not a matter of mere etiquette, and to ignore it can lead to confusion:

> *However, animals acquire CRs at relatively short and long ISIs and also appear to time responses dependent upon the ISI.*[8]

Does this mean that the animals time their responses according to the ISI? Or does it mean that they are timing responses that are dependent on the ISI? Is the timing, or are the responses themselves, "dependent"? (See also CONSISTENT WITH, HIPPOCAMPAL, and INDEPENDENT.)

adverbs, conjunctive. See TRANSITIONAL WORDS AND PHRASES; see also ADDITIONALLY.

adverbs, hyphenation of. See HYPHENATED TERMS.

adverbs, placement of. Adverbs are traditionally said to modify adjectives, verbs, or other adverbs, as well as clauses or whole sentences. Questions regarding the placement of adverbs, however, almost always refer to the position of adverbs such as *only* or *even*, or to the position of adverbs that modify verbs or subject–verb combinations. The following guidelines can be relied on in most instances, but because the grammatical class of adverbs comprises a wide variety, and because adverbs can sometimes occupy any of several positions within a given sentence, no rule regarding their use is likely to be infallible.

If it would change the meaning of a sentence to do otherwise, place *only* or *even* immediately before the word or the phrase that it modifies:

Only 4 subjects participated in Experiment 2.

Four subjects participated only in Experiment 2.

In the first example, the author is obviously interested in the fact that there were 4 subjects only; in the second, the author is stressing that only Experiment 2 had 4 subjects.

An adverb that modifies a single adjective usually precedes it:

The distribution of data is fairly sparse.

The transform is a mathematically accurate representation of the sine wave.

Note that both of these sentences are constructed with the copula (i.e., a form of the verb *to be*) and its complement. In such instances, the adverb usually follows the copula and precedes the complement.

An adverb that modifies a single finite verb can precede it:

Response times significantly decreased.

Usually, however, such an adverb follows the single finite verb:

Response times decreased significantly.

An adverb that modifies a compound verb usually follows the auxiliary or helping verb and precedes the participle or the infinitive:

This has often occurred.

This can often occur.

The adverb can, however, end the sentence or clause instead:

This has occurred often.

This can occur often.

When an adverb modifies a transitive verb and its object, the verb and the object should be construed as a single unit, and the adverb should either precede or follow them:

We briefly presented the instructions.

We presented the instructions briefly.

This rule often applies to infinitives with objects as well. Thus, the first of the following two examples is clearly awkward and less natural than the second:

We wished to further explore this problem.

We wished to explore this problem further.

The verb *to be* can take a participle to express a state of affairs; in such instances, it is simply acting as the copula followed by its complement and the adverb should precede the participle:

This effect is well documented in the literature.

The verb *to be* can also take the past participle to express a transitive action in the passive voice. In such instances, the adverb should follow the participle:

This effect has been documented well by Battaglia.

Thus, the common jargon whereby the adverb precedes the passive use of the participle is incorrect.

Incorrect: *Atypical items are better recognized than typical ones.*
Correct: *Atypical items are recognized better than typical ones.*
Incorrect: *List A is better accessed than List B.*
Correct: *List A is accessed better than List B.*

Note that the passive use of the participle is derived from the active form of the transitive verb: *items are recognized by subjects* is the passive form of the active *subjects recognize items.* To place the adverb before the passive use of the participle would in many instances be to imply that transitive verbs express states rather than actions, which they do not. (See also PASSIVE VOICE.)

Sentence adverbs, which modify whole sentences, may take several positions. The sentence adverb may begin a sentence:

Evidently the Walsh transform is better than the Fourier transform for analyzing certain types of data.

The sentence adverb may also precede the verb:

The Walsh transform evidently is better.

The sentence adverb may even conclude a sentence:

This effect has not been found previously.

Conjunctive adverbs, which link clauses or sentences after the manner of conjunctions, may take any of three positions; their placement is often a matter of style. A conjunctive adverb may begin a sentence, thus:

However, this suggestion is wrong.

It may be placed between the subject and verb:

This suggestion, however, is wrong.

Or it may be placed at the end of the sentence:

This suggestion is wrong, however.

The first of these three examples is typical of most scientific writing; the second occurs rarely, and the third, almost never. Yet one should remember that a conjunctive adverb in the initial position (i.e., as in the first example) often obstructs the reader's progress rather than facilitates it. Words such as *however, nevertheless,* and *therefore* do not usually need to have much attention called to them, and when such a word is tucked away within a sentence rather than loudly broadcasted at the outset, it becomes less obtrusive even as it contributes to the logical continuity of the writer's thought. The writer who always places conjunctive adverbs in the initial position can often seem immature or even childish, and such usages frequently resemble unnecessary rhetorical flag waving. (See TRANSITIONAL WORDS AND PHRASES.)

age, aged. Subjects are not *aged* 25–30 years. This is what the patient oenophile does with only the finest red wines. Subjects are either *25–30 years of age* or *25–30 years old*. Or again, they are *25- to 30-year-old subjects*. If one does not want to use hyphens, the same subjects can be *from 25 to 30 years old*, or *from 25 to 30 years of age*.

agreement. Problems of agreement generally involve numerical correspondences between a subject and a verb, or between a pronoun or a noun and its "antecedent."

Agreement errors of the first type commonly result from material that intervenes between subject and verb; the longer the element that intervenes, the more likely the agreement error. Always in such instances, the true subject is singular, and the intervening material is plural. Thus, in the sentence *Each of the four sets of stimuli were named by one of the four groups of subjects,* the verb has been attracted into the plural by the noun phrase *the four sets of stimuli,* yet neither *sets* nor *stimuli* is the verb's subject. Read: *Each of the four sets of stimuli was named by one of the four groups of subjects.* To keep from making such errors, one must vigilantly identify the grammatical subject and verb of every sentence and clause that one writes. And one must remember that the pronouns *each, every,* and *everyone* always take a verb in the singular.

Another question of agreement between subject and verb arises from the use of collective nouns or pronouns as subjects. In British English, many such words are construed as taking the plural form of the verb, whereas in American usage, they are held to take the singular; *committee, family, group, staff,* and *team* are examples. To the American speaker, the expression *a number of people were in the room* is therefore an exception dictated by this particular use of the word *number,* and exceptions do not make the rule; unlike his or her British counterpart, an American sports commentator would never say, for example, that *the team are on the field.* Nevertheless, perhaps because scientists belong to an international community, many of whose members speak British

English, some scientific writers in America occasionally adopt the British usage. This tendency should be avoided. To write that *the group of 9 mice were placed on the platform* does not accord with American idiom; *the group of 9 mice was placed on the platform* does. Yet another solution is to avoid such quandaries entirely: *The 9 mice were placed on the platform* is correct and concise.

With compound subjects linked by *and,* use the plural verb: *The musical skill of the beginning musician and the verbal facility of the beginning language learner suggest a common attentional scheme.* In the following sentences, the subjects should also be construed as plural: *Both semantic and episodic memory are impaired; color and motion information are affected by the same informational linkage*—in the first sentence, the word *memory* is understood as if it has occurred twice (i.e., *both semantic memory and episodic memory*); in the second, the same is true of the word *information* (i.e., *both color information and motion information*). With compound subjects linked by *or,* however, use the singular verb when both elements of the subject are singular; use the plural verb when both elements of the subject are plural: *On each trial, a picture or a word was presented; in this experiment, pictures or words were presented.*

Errors of agreement between pronouns and antecedents sometimes result from colloquialism (*Everyone has their opinion),* although today they can also reflect the authorial ambiguities instigated by the opponents of "sexist" language. Up until the 1970s, writers were counseled to write *Everyone has his opinion,* letting the masculine pronoun stand for both men and women unless distinctions of gender were important to the discussion at hand. But today, few editors or publishers permit this. The result is the ungainly, although certainly not "sexist," sentence *Everyone has his or her own opinion.* The alternative is to think up other ways of saying the same thing, which is not always difficult: *Most people have their own opinions,* or simply, *People have their own opinions* might do the trick in this case.

Another quandary sometimes arises with respect to the

plural noun subject followed by the plural possessive pronoun as part of an object phrase: Do *subjects raise their hand,* or do *subjects raise their hands?* —with parts of the body, it is usually best to use the plural rather than the singular noun after the plural possessive pronoun; otherwise, the subjects might momentarily be construed as having one hand collectively.

The aforementioned problem does not arise with respect to nouns that are not count nouns: *The subjects restricted their attention to the location of the target* is correct, for example, because *attention* cannot take a plural form (i.e., it is not a count noun). With count nouns, one must rely on one's sense of how the noun might be construed. *The subjects were required to rely on their memory of the target* is correct, for example, because here *memory* does not refer to specific memories isolated for each subject, but rather to memory as a general faculty. In the sentence *The subjects relied on their memories of the event in order to write their descriptions,* on the other hand, the general faculty of memory is not the issue; the specific, individual memories of the subjects are important instead. Likewise, in the sentence *After they had completed the task, the subjects were informed of their mean error rates,* the word *rates* is plural because each rate is specific to each subject, and these rates are not presently being considered in a collective sense.

With parts of the body, in order to avoid problems of number and gender, one can sometimes resort to the definite article instead of the possessive pronoun, in imitation of what is common in most European languages: *The subjects were instructed to press the answer key with the index finger of the right hand.* It is likely, given the current concern about "sexist" language, that American writers will adopt this usage more and more, despite its idiosyncratic nature.

Nouns that express attributes of plural antecedents frequently take the plural, after the pattern of the nouns with the possessive pronouns discussed above: *Bars of different lengths appeared on the screen* (i.e., not *Bars of different length*) is correct. This does not mean that each bar had several lengths, rather that there were several bars, each of which had a given length.

among. *Among* is the preferred form in American English; *amongst* is British idiom. For further remarks on the use of *among*, see BETWEEN.

and. *And* is a coordinating conjunction. It is acceptable to begin a sentence with *and*, although as with any stylistic device, this one should not be overused. The same is true of *but, nor, or,* and *yet.* Particularly the initial *but* and *yet* are to be recommended as occasional substitutes for *however* at the start of a sentence, if only for the sake of stylistic variety. For punctuation with *and*, see *Commas and coordination*, under COMMAS. For further remarks, see COORDINATION.

ANOVA. This is one of the most common abbreviations used by experimental psychologists. It is the universal acronym for *analysis of variance,* a statistical means of analyzing and evaluating the variability of data in terms of the possible effects or interactions of contributing variables or factors. The acronym *ANOVA* seems to work best as a count noun (i.e., a noun that has both singular and plural forms); that is, it seems best to spell the expression out to refer to the general concept of analysis of variance, and to restrict the acronym to usages such as an ANOVA, the ANOVA, or, in the plural, ANOVAs. To say that ANOVA of the data revealed the following significant effects sounds stilted; it is better to say that an ANOVA or ANOVAs revealed them.

Writers differ with regard to the idiomatic use of the term ANOVA. One author will refer to an ANOVA for the data; another will write of an ANOVA on the data; yet another will prefer an ANOVA of the data. Common sense, however, suggests that since both analysis and variance usually take complements introduced by the preposition of, so too should their acronym. If we carry out an ANOVA of the peak latency of conditioned responses, we obtain the variance of these responses, and we undertake an analysis of that variance. We may of course perform or conduct an ANOVA on the data, in which case the preposition is governed by the verb rather than the acronym, but having done so, we will still *have* performed *an analysis of* them. Note too that to speak of *an ANOVA analysis* is redundant; it is the same as saying *an analysis of variance analysis.*

As for the hyphenation of terms that frequently accompany the acronym *ANOVA,* one should remember this pattern: a three-way repeated measures ANOVA.

apostrophes. Apart from the occasional forgivable slip, there is no good reason for misusing apostrophes. Here are five rules, accompanied by a sixth admonition:

1. Singular nouns take the possessive apostrophe before the "s": each student's response. Plural nouns take the possessive apostrophe after the "s": students' responses.

2. Never confuse the possessive apostrophe with the plural; that is, never write patient's with Hodgkin's disease instead of patients with Hodgkin's disease.

3. Learn the distinction between its (possessive) and it's ("it is"), and do not forget it; there is no excuse for confusing these forms other than in making the inadvertent typographical error. Recall that its is a third person possessive pronoun; one would never make the mistake of writing her's or hi's, so why should one ever confuse its with it's ?

4. At the end of proper names that end in "s," one should probably follow Strunk and White's advice by adding not only the possessive apostrophe but also the "s": write Jones's, or Stevens's, not Jones' or *Stevens'* (the name Jesus, however, is an exception; here, simply add the apostrophe: *Jesus'*). Awkward although this usage may be, more editors and publishers seem to advocate it than not.

5. Use the possessive apostrophe with the gerund (the verbal noun ending in *–ing*) to distinguish it from the present

participle (the verbal adjective ending in *–ing*). This rule, the application of which is fairly simple, is uncongenial to some writers, who are likely to object if anyone suggests adding the apostrophe to any gerund in their text. But the distinction is neither stylistic nor pedantic. If one writes that *this effect depends on the subject predicting the shape of the target,* one is saying that the effect depends on the particular subject, who merely happens to be predicting the target's shape at the same time; this is because *predicting* will be construed as a participle modifying the noun *subject*. The same meaning is expressed in the sentence *This effect depends on the subject who is predicting the shape of the target.* If one writes, on the other hand, that *this effect depends on the subject's predicting the shape of the target,* one is saying that the effect depends on whether or not the subject indeed predicts the target's shape; *predicting* will be construed as a gerund. Thus, in the first example, the subject is what matters; in the latter one, the prediction is important. Surely the latter alternative is the only logical choice.

The following examples will perhaps help:

This is shown by the sum having the same rank ordering.

This sentence literally means, *This is shown by the sum with the same rank ordering,* or, *This is shown by the sum that has the same rank ordering.* In either case, the sum is the topic of interest.

This is shown by the sum's having the same rank ordering.

This sentence, on the other hand, means, *This is shown by the fact that the sum has the same rank ordering.* That is, the fact of having the same ordering is the topic of interest.

These examples show that the use of the apostrophe with the gerund is a matter of logic and clarity, not of style or of how something "looks" in print.

6. When it is possible to use the apostrophe as a means of ridding the language of unnecessary jargon, do so. *Subject*

reaction times should therefore be *the subjects' reaction times; the sound source location* should be *the sound source's location; memory for high school classmate pictures* should be *memory for high school classmates' pictures;* and *naloxone enhancement of freezing* should be *naloxone's enhancement of freezing.* Such revisions help to combat the stylistic tendency variously known in style and usage handbooks as nominalization, noun plague, or noun rubbish. (See NOUNS AND NOMINALIZATION; STYLE.)

as. To many writers, the use of *as* instead of *since* or *because* sounds awkward or stilted; even though this word is only two letters long, it smacks of the turgid jargon of bureaucrats. The first objection to the causal use of *as* is therefore a matter of stylistic taste, and the writer who employs it runs the risk of alienating at least some readers. A second reason sometimes given for avoiding the causal *as* is that it tends to trivialize the cause that follows: *The students were told to pay close attention to the material, as it was to be on the test later.* Surely, *The students were told to pay close attention to the material, because it was to be on the test later* stresses the cause more emphatically; indeed in this instance, the instructor's emphasis on what the students were to do is essential. A third reason to avoid the causal *as* is that because *as* can also mean "while" or "when," it can be momentarily confusing: *This pattern was representative of rats receiving signaled and unsignaled shock, as records for these two groups were virtually indistinguishable.*[9] Although by the end of this sentence the reader knows that *as* does indeed mean "because," one cannot be sure of this interpretation until the sentence is complete. The causal *as* thus may not lead to an ultimate misreading, but it can create a temporarily unresolved ambiguity that *because* or *since* will always prevent. The judicious writer should therefore choose *since* or *because* instead of *as* whenever possible and should use *as* to mean "while" carefully.

Those who still insist on resorting to the causal use of *as,* however, should remember the following principle: without the comma, *as* is more likely to be construed as "while"; with the comma, it is more likely to be construed as "since" or "because." Compare the following sentences: *The students were told to pay close attention to the material as they would be tested on it later* ("while"). *The students were told to pay close attention to the material, as they would be tested on it later* ("because").

as shown. It is better to write *As is shown in Figure 1...* than to write *As shown in Figure 1...* The awkward *as shown* presumably reflects the interests of stylistic economy, whereby the verbal passive (*as is shown*) has been shortened through the removal of the finite form of the verb *to be* —namely, *is*. But by removing the finite verb, the writer leaves the reader wondering what verb is in fact meant: *is, was,* or *has been* are all possibilities, depending on the context. This is the same as writing *as discovered* instead of *as is discovered [every day], as was discovered [during the early years of this century],* or *as has been discovered [recently]; as stated* instead of *as is, was, or has been stated;* or *as done in the 19th century* instead of *as was done in the 19th century.* In each case the complete, rather than the abbreviated, form of the verb is preferable.

as to. There is no need to use the expression *as to* with nouns such as *information, debate,* or *question. Information about the function of a system* is clearer and more straightforward than *information as to the function of the system; debate about the system's function* is more direct than *debate as to* that function, which is circumlocutious. Likewise, *questions as to whether* can usually be *questions of whether, questions about whether,* or, simply, *questions whether. Reasons as to why* are *reasons why.* The expression *as to,* although not wrong, is often either pretentious or evasive; whenever this might be the case, *as to* should be avoided.

avoid. In modern English, *avoid* is by convention a transitive verb that takes a personal subject; it means "to keep away from, to prevent [something] from occurring, to refrain from, to evade or escape [something]": *With this procedure, we could avoid the occurrence of both ceiling and floor effects. By taking precautions, we avoided what appeared to be certain danger.* To let an impersonal construction function as the subject of *avoid* is thus to engage in PERSONIFICATION, which writers who are not novelists or poets should themselves avoid unless they wish to achieve a specific aesthetic effect. Thus "procedures" do not themselves "avoid" anything; researchers design their procedures in order to avoid something that can confound their results. Likewise, "tasks" do not "avoid" confounding factors; the careful "planning" of experiments does not "avoid" undue stress among experimental subjects; and "stimuli" of a certain type cannot "avoid" inducing specific illusions. *Experimenters* design tasks, plan experiments, and present stimuli, and when they do so, they, and not their experiments, tasks, or stimuli, attempt to avoid any potentially confounding factors or unwanted effects.

B

based on, on the basis of. These two expressions, although frequently confused in contemporary idiom, actually differ in meaning and in grammatical function when they are used correctly. *Based* is the past participle of the verb *to base*. *Based on* comprises the past participle plus the preposition that introduces its complement *(this argument is based on fact; an argument based on fact)*. *On the basis of,* however, functions as a preposition that introduces adverbial phrases or clauses. Thus it is correct to write, *The present study is based on previous work done in our laboratory,* or to refer to *work [that is] based on previous studies;* but it is incorrect to write, *Based on the results of Experiment 1, we expected that subjects would display longer latencies in Experiment 2.* In the latter case, only *on the basis of* can be correct, for *we* are certainly not based on the results of Experiment 1; the opening phrase properly modifies the whole clause that follows, not its subject, and the adverbial phrase, not the participial phrase, is appropriate. If I design an experiment *on the basis of previous studies* (adverbial phrase), my act of designing the experiment is *based on those studies* (participial phrase). If, on the other hand, I design an experiment *based on previous studies,* the experiment itself, not my act of designing it, is based on them. The misuse of *based on* as an adverbial construction is a specific instance of the current general tendency to confuse adverbs and adjectives (see ADVERBS VERSUS ADJECTIVES).

be. See SUBJUNCTIVE.

because. As a conjunction, the word *because* introduces a subordinate or dependent clause that expresses a reason or reasons for what is presented in an independent clause in the same sentence. This subordinate clause can either precede or follow the independent clause; there is nothing wrong with using *because* to begin the sentence. Clauses with the word *because,* however, do not appear to be frequent in scientific writing. *As* is common in its place; *since* is less frequent; and *because* and the coordinating conjunction *for* seem almost never to occur. The reason, perhaps, is that of all the conjunctions that express causality, *because* is usually felt to be the strongest and most emphatic; and most scientific writers tend to present their results and conclusions provisionally, as small parts of a much larger picture that no single experiment or set of experiments can decisively confirm or deny. Nevertheless, since the word *because* is so direct, emphatic, and concrete, one should at least attempt to use it whenever it might be appropriate. *Because* may contain more letters than *as,* but its meaning is undeniably more concise.

When a clause with *because* begins a sentence—that is, when it precedes the independent clause to which it is linked—it is set off by a comma:

> *Because both processes produce the correct answer, errors must be attributed to some spurious process that races against the correct response and beats it.*[10]

Clauses with *because* that follow the independent clause are either restrictive or nonrestrictive. The restrictive clause so defines, limits, or restricts the meaning of the preceding independent clause that it cannot be removed without changing the independent clause's meaning. It is therefore considered essential to the meaning of the sentence, and it is not set off by a comma:

> *We selected this apparatus because it was inexpensive.*

The nonrestrictive clause, on the other hand, is not essential to the meaning of the sentence; if it is removed, the meaning of the independent clause will not be changed. The nonrestrictive clause therefore takes the comma:

> *This was not the optimal condition for the assessment of such differences, because the data were obtained in large trial blocks.*

See also *Commas with nonrestrictive, as opposed to restrictive, modifiers,* and *Commas and subordination: Adverbial clauses.*

between. The preposition *between,* when it does not occur as part of a compound adjective, takes either a plural noun or a pair of nouns as its complement: *Pair type was varied between subjects; subjects discriminated between Stimulus A and Stimulus B.* Therefore, one cannot say that *Subjects discriminated between a pair* or that there are *differences between performance on implicit and explicit memory.* Subjects either discriminate between the two elements that make up a pair, or between one pair and another; and the aforementioned differences presumably occur between performance on implicit memory and performance on explicit memory. Likewise, one cannot say that *between each trial, the rat was removed from the test box,* because this could only have happened *between trials.*

As for the notion that *between* should be used for only two things and *among* for three or more, this rarely presents any real difficulty: the phrases *between subjects* and *between groups,* for example, do not at all suggest that only two subjects or groups are involved. It is true that *among* can never signify two things only, and that for only two things, *between* must be used. But *between* is also correct when a comparison is made between each thing and each of the other things with which it is associated; *variance between groups* thus refers to the variance between each group and each of the other groups being investigated, not to variance between two groups. *Variance among groups* would be less appropriate, because the groups are not really being considered together as a single, larger whole.

When *between* introduces a phrase that complements a preceding noun, it should follow that noun immediately. To call a test in which subjects must choose between saccharin and water *a choice test between saccharin and water* is incorrect; the choice, not the test, is between saccharin and water.

between group, within group; between-group, within-group. *Between-group variance* is the variance that occurs because of measured differences between groups of subjects; it represents the degree to which groups or conditions differ from one another. *Within-group variance* is the variance that occurs because of measured differences within groups of subjects. These terms take the hyphen only when they are used as compound adjectives before the noun: *between-group variance,* but *variance between groups; within-group variance,* but *variance within a group.* Note that the plural "s" is not necessary with either expression when it precedes the noun that it modifies. Because the word *between* implies the plural, the compound adjective *between-group* implies more than one group; consider, as analogies, *a five-man crew, a 3-hour exam,* and *a multiple-choice test*. As for *within-group,* since the variance occurs within a single group or within each of several single groups, again the plural "s" is not needed. See, however, BETWEEN SUBJECTS.

between subject[s], within subjects; between-subject[s], within-subjects. The hyphen is included only when these terms act as compound adjectives before the noun: *between-subject design, between-subject factors, within-subjects design, within-subjects factors*. Since there will always be more than one such subject, and since the word *between* always implies the plural, one can leave out the "s" in *between-subject,* just as in the phrase *between-group variance*. Likewise, one may be tempted to drop the "s" and write of a *within-subject factor* and *within-subject factors*. But this is not analogous to the form *within-group variance,* because a within-subjects factor is not a factor that exists within a single subject. It is rather a factor on which all subjects are tested, just as a between-subject factor is a factor on which only some subjects are tested. A question then arises: If *within-subjects* must always take the "s" to prevent ambiguity, would it be better, in the interests of consistency, to retain the "s" on *between-subjects* as well? This is certainly a simple and acceptable solution, although in the plural it becomes hard to enunciate: *between-subjects factors* is harder to pronounce than *between-subject factors.*

Some authors attempt to let the form of the adjective depend on the number of the noun: *between-subjects factor, between-subject factors, between-subjects design, between-subject designs*. This pattern is interesting, but peculiar; in English, we never refer to *a multiple-choices test* in the singular, as opposed to *multiple-choice tests* in the plural. One should choose either *between-subject* or *between-subjects* and stick to it. But *within-subjects* should always stand in the plural.

both, adjective. The adjective *both* means "the two," as in *both protocols, both tasks, both subjects*. In all of these instances, the protocols, tasks, and subjects must already have been mentioned in the text for the use of *both* to be understandable. One could also correctly write *both of the protocols, both of the tasks, both of the subjects,* but this would not be necessary; just as with *all of the subjects, all the subjects,* and *all subjects,* the difference is largely one of style rather than matter. Before the pronoun in the objective case, however, *of the* is required: *both of us, both of them* (cf. all of them).

Confusion sometimes arises with regard to the modifiers that accompany the plural noun following *both:* Does one write *both types of task,* or *both types of tasks?* As with *these types of task* and *these types of tasks,* either form is acceptable.

both...and. This construction is useful, but it can lead to problems of parallelism: *Both Jones and Francis (1975) and Smith (1989) found that....* In this example, the reader at first construes *both...and* to link Jones and Francis; the second use of *and* then comes as a surprise. *Not only Jones and Francis (1975) but also Smith (1989)...* might work, depending on what the author is trying to say; another possibility would be to reverse the names of the authors: *Both Smith (1989) and Jones and Francis (1975)...* It is likely, however, that the author wished to keep these studies in chronological order, so that the simplest solution would be to delete *both: Jones and Francis (1975) and Smith (1989)....* One need not use *both...and* at all unless it is necessary for clarity.

As with the correlative conjunctions *either...or, neither...nor,* and *not only...but also,* the constructions that follow *both* and *and* must be grammatically parallel. It is thus wrong to write of *both the massed and distributed presentations;* to preserve the parallelism, one must write *both the massed and the distributed presentations.* Note that here the use of *both...and* does appear to make the meaning clear—*the massed and distributed presentations,* for example, would be self-contradictory, because it would suggest that the presentations were both massed and distributed at the same time. But *the massed and the distributed presentations* could suffice too, for the repetition of *the* would suggest that two different groups of presentations were being discussed. Once the originally faulty parallelism has been made clear, the inclusion of *both* in this example is largely a matter of stylistic emphasis.

One must also be careful not to confuse the adjective *both,* meaning "the two," with the coordinating use of *both* in *both...and,* as can occur whenever the noun that follows *both* is plural: *We found both significant effects of letter similarity and of color similarity.* Here the reader will at once construe *both significant effects* to refer to "the two significant effects," as if they have already been under discussion, but the sentence subsequently turns out to be a construction with *both...and* instead. Read: *We found significant effects of both letter similarity and color similarity.* Or, again, *both* could be dropped: *We found significant effects of letter similarity and color similarity.*

Note, finally, that the following is incorrect: *in both spatial working memory as well as reference memory.* The proper construction always consists of *both...and,* never *both...as well as.* Here, the simplest solution would be to omit the word *both: in spatial working memory as well as reference memory.*

brain. Many scientific writers tend to omit the definite article from constructions that require it in daily speech or in other types of formal written English; in the field of neuroscience, for example, the definite article is often elided before mention of parts of the brain. It is thus common to find *in bregma, in parietal cortex, in hippocampus,* or *in rat brain,* instead of *in the bregma, in the parietal cortex, in the hippocampus,* or *in the rat's brain.* These are examples of jargon, or language shared by members of a particular profession. There is a difference, however, between jargon that is necessary because new ideas or discoveries require new locutions for their expression, and jargon that is gratuitous. The omission of the definite article in the four instances just given seems to represent the latter, because there appears to be no reason why it should be left out. In fact, there are good reasons for its use. First, common English idiom recommends it. Second, even neuroscientists who studiously attempt to avoid the definite article usually do so inconsistently, so that what is *parietal cortex* in one sentence or paragraph will be *the parietal cortex* in another. This suggests that such writers do not care that much about the definite article's presence or absence, and that they use it randomly. Third, *brain* is not a generic substance like food or drink, and the expression *in brain* is odd at best. In my opinion, the definite article should be left in wherever daily speech or formal written English would dictate it; if, however, one insists on leaving it out, one should at least do so consistently (see under THE).

but. *But* is a coordinating conjunction. Unlike *and*, which can link not only pairs but series of words, phrases, or clauses, *but* links only two such elements. Sometimes *but* links words or phrases: *The two paradigms provide different but compatible information regarding the processing of interacting dimensions.*[11] Usually, however, *but* links clauses: *The limitation to American authors results in a somewhat parochial view that automatically excludes much that is of interest in schizophrenia research, but the exclusion is understandable because APPA is an American organization.*[12] When thus used to coordinate clauses, *but* should be preceded by a comma. Unlike *and*, *but* rarely links a compound verb (one subject with two verbs)—although it may be used thus for concise aesthetic effect: *They fought the skirmish well but lost the battle.* Such an example, however, is unlikely to form a pattern for much scientific prose.

Another acceptable, although infrequent, use of *but* occurs at the beginning of a sentence: *Such awareness, however, did not affect how they spelled homophones, in view of the fact that spelling performance did not reliably differ according to mood. But attention to the biased meanings of homophones would serve as a second processing trial for the targets and make them more perspicuous on the recognition test.*[13] Or again, more simply: *But the interaction was not significant. But* can provide an elegant means of transition, and it is sometimes stylistically preferable to *however* because it is less obtrusive. See also AND.

C

cannot, can't. *Cannot* should be written as one word, not two. *Can't*, which is an informal contraction of *cannot*, should be avoided in formal prose unless one wishes to achieve a colloquial effect for some specific rhetorical purpose. In a paper of 5–10 pages, such an effect would likely be compromised by the use of can't more than once or twice. In scientific prose, therefore, *cannot* is almost always the best choice.

cf. *Cf.* is the abbreviation for the Latin *confer* (English "compare"), which is the imperative form of the verb *conferre* ("to compare"). *Cf.* therefore does *not* mean "see"—a term that needs no abbreviated form: *(see, e.g., Treisman & Gelade, 1980; Treisman & Gormican, 1988)*. See also ABBREVIATIONS, LATIN; E.G.; I.E.; and SEE.

collinear. *Collinear* is an adjective, not an adverb. On this distinction, see ADVERBS VERSUS ADJECTIVES.

colons. In modern American usage, the colon marks a full stop and refers the reader to what follows. The colon is thus preceded by a relatively general statement and followed by complementary material that develops or explains that statement through further specification or presentation of greater detail. The general statement almost always consists of an independent clause or a sentence; the subsequent material may take the form of a word, phrase, or clause; a series of words, phrases, or clauses; a sentence of any type; or indented material such as quotations or mathematical formulas, as in the examples given here.

In the following example, the general statement introduces

a theory; the ensuing sentence fleshes it out:

> Kanwisher (1986, 1987) offered the following account of repetition
> blindness: Even though the second instance of a repeated word is
> recognized as a type, it is not individuated as a distinct token when
> it occurs too soon after the first instance.[14]

Some may wonder why the sentence after the colon in this example begins with an uppercase letter. Unfortunately, there is no adequate rule. The argument for capitalization is that the sentence after the colon is complete in itself and could easily stand alone; therefore it should begin as all sentences do, with a capital letter. The argument against capitalization is that this sentence completes the meaning of the sentence that precedes it; it is a continuation of that sentence, and it therefore should not begin with a capital letter. Both arguments are good; neither is better than the other. Editorial policy is likely to rule in such instances, unless an author is adamant.

All writers would agree, however, that if the sentence after the colon is a question in direct address, it must begin with the capital letter:

> This state of affairs raises the basic question: What new principles
> and mechanisms are needed to understand how multiple sources of
> visual information preattentively cooperate to generate a percept of
> three-dimensional (3D) form?[15]

If, on the other hand, the colon is followed by words, phrases, or dependent clauses, the ensuing material will surely begin in lowercase, as in the following example that contains a list:

> Four sequential pairs of 2.5-sec light and tone stimuli were pre-
> sented: light-light, tone-tone, light-tone, and tone-light.[16]

Note that the short phrases in the preceding list are separated by commas. In lists that consist of longer phrases or clauses, it is usually best to separate the items not with commas, but with semicolons. This will always be the case if any of the elements of the list contain internal punctuation such as commas or dashes:

> *The average weights were the following: Bird 111, 432g; Bird 136, 488g; and Bird 168, 428g.*[17]

One final piece of advice (here introduced by the unusual phrase, rather than the usual sentence, followed by a colon): Read each sentence that contains a colon carefully; ask yourself whether or not it really does point to something that follows. If not, a semicolon will probably be called for instead; see SEMICOLONS.

commas. The initial rule so often cited with respect to the use of the comma—that one should use a comma if one needs to pause for breath—is seldom adequate. To begin with, people's senses vary; where some will feel the need to pause in a sentence, others will not. More importantly, several of the rules for the use of commas follow the conventional logic of written prose, not the biological necessities of human respiration. Here are a few guidelines that are particularly relevant to scientific writing:[18]

Commas with Appositives. Appositives rename what has gone before; in most instances, they are set off by commas:

> *Recently, elevation of brain histamine levels by metoprine, <u>an inhibitor of the histamine-degrading enzyme histamine-N-methyltransferase</u>, was found to inhibit maximal hindleg extension after electroshock in the rat.*[19]

If the appositive construction would be ambiguous with commas—if, for example, it might at first be construed as part of a series rather than as an appositive—or if it contains internal punctuation, use dashes instead:

> *Information concerning the two dimensions of the line—texture and slant—could be obtained from the same location.*[20]

Commas and Coordination: Compound Sentences and Cmpound Verbs or Predicates. The following incorrectly punctuated sentence contains a coordinated construction typical of much scientific writing:

> All <u>subjects</u> <u>were recruited</u> *from the department of psychology subject pool,* <u>and</u> <u>received</u> *course credit for participation.*

Note that the sentence contains one subject (*subjects*) and two verbs (*were recruited, received*), and that they are linked with *and,* which is preceded by a comma. This use of the comma differs from what is recommended in almost all handbooks on English grammar and usage. Standard usage follows the rule that a single subject and two verbs linked by *and* (i.e., a *compound verb or predicate*) do not take the comma before *and,* whereas a subject and verb linked by *and* to yet another subject and verb (i.e., a *compound sentence*) do take the comma before *and.* If this standard usage is to be followed, the writer of the sentence above has therefore two choices:

> All <u>subjects</u> <u>were recruited</u> *from the department of psychology subject pool and* <u>received</u> *course credit for participation.*
>
> (compound verb)

> All <u>subjects</u> <u>were recruited</u> *from the department of psychology subject pool,* <u>and</u> <u>they</u> <u>received</u> *course credit for participation.*
>
> (compound sentence)

Of these choices, the second is better, because the verbs *were recruited* and *received* are not parallel; *were recruited* is in the passive voice, whereas *received* is in the active voice. The reader of the first is therefore likely to stumble, wondering whether *were* is implied before *received* as well, which of course turns out not to be the case. Yet either alternative is better than the original.

Why so many scientific writers tend to prefer the original sentence just given to the other two is not entirely clear, although at least two possibilities suggest themselves. On the one hand, the writer of such a sentence may sense that it contains a compound verb, yet at the same time, this writer may think that the clause before *and* is so long or so complete that it requires a pause, which is then signified with the added comma. This is an example in which the assumption that the comma represents a pause for breath has erroneously been allowed to prevail over the conventional rule. On the other hand, the writer may sense that the sentence should be a compound sentence with two subjects and verbs, but the writer may fear to use the pronoun as the subject of the second clause because pronouns seem somehow ambiguous. With respect to the aforementioned sentence, neither of these reasons can adequately justify the deviation from convention. Too many readers will assume that the comma followed by *and* signals the end of an independent clause and that the next word or phrase will begin another independent clause that follows. If a verb without a subject ensues instead, the reader will stumble, backtrack, and reread the sentence to find out how the author wishes it to be construed. No reader should have to do this.

In fact there are still other alternatives to the first sentence just given, in which one does not resort to the comma at all:

> All <u>subjects</u> <u>were recruited</u> from the department of psychology subject pool; <u>they</u> <u>received</u> course credit for participation.
> (compound sentence, with semicolon instead of *and*)

> All <u>subjects</u> <u>were recruited</u> from the department of psychology subject pool. <u>They</u> <u>received</u> course credit for participation.
>   (two sentences)

The writer is urged to consider choosing either of these possibilities, again because the passive form *were recruited* and the active form *received* are not parallel.

In the following examples of coordinations with commas, the subjects and verbs are underlined, and the punctuation is correct:

This <u>result</u> <u>replicates</u> and <u>extends</u> the results of Bouton (1986, Experiment 2).[21]

(subject with compound verb; no comma is necessary)

Our primary <u>interest</u> in this study <u>was</u> to examine whether or not motion perception was experienced, and <u>we</u> therefore <u>did</u> not <u>ask</u> the observers to report different types of motion.[22]

(compound sentence; *and* is preceded by the comma)

What <u>do</u> <u>models</u> <u>do</u>, and what <u>can</u> <u>they</u> not <u>do</u>?[23]

(compound sentence; *and* is preceded by the comma)

Apart from the use of *and,* similar coordinations are also constructed with *but, for, nor, or,* and *yet.* The use of *for* is simple: it is a good substitute for *since* or *because,* it can never begin a sentence, and it is always preceded by the comma:

This task represents a more accurate test of spatial memory, for in it the confound of working memory effects has been eliminated.

But and *yet* occur only rarely with compound verbs; one should not use them thus unless one seeks a terseness uncommon in scientific prose: *They fought well but lost.* Otherwise, when either *but* or *yet* coordinates two independent clauses, it should be preceded by the comma:

Several hypotheses involving error correction were considered, but none was consistent with the results of this experiment.

Or can work with both compound verbs and compound sentences; *nor* is likely to be used in a compound sentence only, but the subject and verb will be inverted after it in a manner that usually seems too literary for scientific discourse:

There were no significant effects of any of the variables, nor were there any interactions between them.

Compound sentences may also be coordinated with conjunctive adverbs such as *however, nevertheless, nonetheless, thus,* and so forth. For this purpose, commas alone should not be used; the adverb must be preceded by a semicolon and followed by a comma. If not, as in the following example, the reader will not know whether the adverb goes with the preceding or with the ensuing clause:

> *Several studies have addressed the distribution of SP-LI within the human pons and medulla, however, the only detailed description of the distribution of substance P fibre and terminal immunoreactivity within the brainstem is in the rat* [sic].[24]

Note that if *however* completes the meaning of the clause that precedes it, then it signifies a contrast with something that has been said in a preceding sentence; if it is construed as introducing the second clause, then it marks a contrast between the second clause and the first in the sentence at hand. If the semicolon is used in place of the first comma, there can be no ambiguity about this; *however* can then only introduce the contrast between the second clause and the first. In most English handbooks, the erroneous substitution of the comma for the semicolon in compound sentences is called, variously, a *comma splice,* a *run-on sentence,* or a *run-together sentence.*

Commas with For Example or That Is. When *for example* or *that is* acts as as a transitional phrase that opens a sentence, it is set off by a comma:

> *For example, proprioception alone may indicate one spatial direction, whereas vision alone may indicate a second spatial direction.*[25]

If *for example* or *that is* introduces a shift of thought embedded within a sentence, it is still followed by the comma, but the entire construction is set off by dashes (em-dashes, in the typesetter's vocabulary):

> *An image of an object—for example, of a box, a plant, or a chair— replaced the image of the person in the matching slide.*

If *for example* or *that is* begins the second of two independent clauses, it is preceded by a semicolon and followed by the comma. This sentence illustrates both of the preceding principles:

> *The assumption is that if the subject can separate trials—that is, if trial end is made distinct in some way—the current-trial buffer would be cleared at the end of a trial; that is, working memory processing would cease as long as trial end is clearly demarcated.*[26]

When *for example* or *that is* introduces an afterthought at the end of a sentence, it is preceded by a dash and followed by the comma:

> *For each subject, we derived congruity scores—that is, the arithmetical reaction time (RT) difference between sounds having congruent attributes and those having incongruent attributes.*[27]

Commas with Nonrestrictive, as Opposed to Restrictive, Modifiers. Restrictive modifiers limit the meaning of what precedes them; nonrestrictive modifiers do not. If one writes that *the psychologist B.F. Skinner taught at Harvard,* one is implying that there are many psychologists, but that Skinner is the psychologist whom one is talking about, as opposed to all the rest. Were one to remove *B.F. Skinner* from the sentence, one would change the meaning of the sentence entirely. Thus, the name *B.F. Skinner* is here a modifier that restricts the meaning of the word *psychologist*—it is a restrictive modifier—and it is therefore not set off by commas. If one writes, on the other hand, that *B.F. Skinner, the psychologist, taught at Harvard,* one is of course implying that there was only one B.F. Skinner, who happened to be a psychologist. One could remove the phrase *the psychologist* from the sentence without changing the sentence's meaning. Thus, the phrase *the psychologist* is here a modifier that does not restrict the meaning of the name *B.F. Skinner*—it is a nonrestrictive modifier—and it is therefore set off by commas.

Nonrestrictive modifiers, commas:

C.W. Eriksen, the editor, teaches psychology at Illinois; B.A. Eriksen, the novelist, is his wife.

Restrictive modifiers, no commas:

Eriksen the editor teaches psychology at Illinois; Eriksen the novelist is his wife.

Commas with Opening Phrases. Scientific writers like to begin sentences with introductory phrases, which often contribute a transition of thought:

In three experiments, we explored the effects of…

According to the model of intermodal pattern perception, the capacity of the visual and tactile perceptual systems is limited by…

Using binocular vision, each subject fixated…

It is safe to say that in all three of these instances, more writers would include commas than not, but that particularly with respect to the first sentence, there might be some disagreement. If one were to peruse a variety of books and articles in quest of introductory phrases, one would soon discover that the opening prepositional phrase in the first sentence may or may not take the comma, depending on authorial or editorial preference (one can never be sure which is responsible). Some writers almost never use commas with such phrases; others insist on them. Still others will choose to use the comma with the prepositional phrase or not, depending on the exigencies of rhythm and style. Note that if the comma is there, one will pause when reading the sentence; if the comma is removed, one will be likely to read on through, without pausing. In either case, the meaning will remain the same, but the sentence will have a different rhythm, which may depend on the larger context of which it is a part. Whether or not one includes the comma in this instance, the editor's word will probably rule in the matter. As for the second and third sentences—there is not nearly so much to be said; introductory -*ing* phrases should almost always take the comma, unless they are followed immediately by a finite verb:

> *More promising is the attempt to determine the mechanics with which animals distinguish between simple and complex visual stimuli.*

Comma Placement and Meaning. Sometimes the location or the presence or absence of a comma can change the meaning of a sentence completely:

> *When the frame enclosed the word only, the space inside the frame was relevant.*

> *When the frame enclosed the word, only the space inside the frame was relevant.*

Commas in Series. In a series of three or more parallel items, commas separate the items; when the last two items in the series are joined by a coordinating conjunction, the conjunction is preceded by a comma. Two parallel items joined by a coordinating conjunction, on the other hand, do not take the comma:

> *As is apparent, there is a conspicuous alignment of patterns, with A, B, and C on the right end of the axis and D and E on the left.*[28]

In this example, A, B, and C constitute a series, so the comma precedes *and*. D and E, however, constitute a pair, as do A, B, and C plus D and E, so in both of these instances, no comma precedes *and*.

Note that *either* is not used in such a series with *or*, because the series contains more than two elements:

> *Each response was scored as a hit, a miss, a correct rejection, or a false alarm.*[29]

In the following sentence, *An initial analysis of the results included case at test (uppercase vs. lowercase), test rate (30 vs. 35 ms), frequency in the language (high vs. low) and study condition (uppercase, lowercase, or no study) as factors,*[30] there is really no reason to justify the absence of the series comma. There are four sets of factors; all are of equal grammatical and semantic weight, and they are reasonably parallel; the comma should be added following the parenthesis before *and*.

Commas Between Subjects and Verbs. A *single* comma may never divide subject and verb. This is true no matter how long the unit of the sentence that constitutes the subject may be. The following sentence contains such an error:

> *Motor limbic seizures including upper extremity clonus, rearing and occasional falling, occurred approximately 30 min after pilocarpine injection.*[31]

Note that the subject includes everything before the verb *occurred.* If the phrase *including upper extremity clonus, rearing, and occasional falling* is meant to be restrictive, the comma before the verb should be removed and the series comma should be placed before *and:*

> *Motor limbic seizures including upper extremity clonus, rearing, and occasional falling occurred approximately 30 min after pilocarpine injection.*

If, on the other hand, the phrase *including upper extremity clonus, rearing, and occasional falling* is meant to be nonrestrictive, and hence parenthetical, a comma should be added after *seizures,* and the series comma should again be placed before *and;* but the comma after *falling* should remain, for it now no longer separates subject from verb but rather ends the nonrestrictive phrase:

> *Motor limbic seizures, including upper extremity clonus, rearing, and occasional falling, occurred approximately 30 min after pilocarpine injection.*

Commas and Subordination: Adverbial Clauses. Adverbial clauses, when they precede the independent clause that they modify, are followed by the comma. If an adverbial clause introduces the second independent clause in a compound sentence, it is also followed by the comma, but it is not preceded by a comma unless it is parenthetical. The following sentence illustrates both principles:

> *When two noise pips were presented bilaterally but simultaneously, a single auditory event was located in the center of the head, and when the pip in one ear led the other by just 1 msec, the sound shifted unequivocally to the leading ear.*[32]

A restrictive adverbial clause that follows the independent clause that it modifies is not set off by a comma:

> *In fact, immediate reinforcement and delayed reinforcement of either 3 or 9 sec produced comparable response rates when only the first .5 sec of the delay interval was signaled; responding was reduced substantially when the entire 3- or 9-sec delay interval was unsignaled.*[33]

Thus, in the following two examples, the comma is crucial:

Restrictive: *The dot patterns were superimposed so that the common dots coincided.*

Nonrestrictive: *The dot patterns were superimposed, so that the common dots coincided.*

In the restrictive example, the coinciding of the common dots is the reason why the patterns were superimposed; the result clause expresses the experimenter's purpose. In the nonrestrictive example, the coinciding of the dots simply happens to occur because the patterns were superimposed; this coincidental result does not necessarily have anything to do with the experimenter's purpose.

Commas with Transitional Words. Transitional words that open a sentence tend to take the comma if they have more than two syllables: *however, nevertheless, nonetheless*. If they have only one or two syllables, the comma tends to be more optional: *hence, indeed, therefore, thus*. In either case, the choice often depends on the stylistic rhythm one seeks. Yet sometimes, the role of the comma can determine meaning. *Thus*, for example, can express subtle nuances: with the comma, it is more likely to mean "as a result"; without the comma, it is more likely to mean "in this way," "in this manner." Sometimes too, the omission of the comma can permit an initial ambiguity in how a sentence should be read; compare the following examples:

> *Still these researchers' procedure seems efficient.*
>
> *Still, these researchers' procedure seems efficient.*
>
> *Specifically iboteneate lesions of the hippocampus with extensive loss of cells in the subiculum impaired the rats' performance.*
>
> *Specifically, iboteneate lesions of the hippocampus with extensive loss of cells in the subiculum impaired the rats' performance.*
>
> *Rather male courtship behavior stimulates ovarian growth.*
>
> *Rather, male courtship behavior stimulates ovarian growth.*

(See also COORDINATION.)

comparison. In psychology experiments, behavior is observed and measured under specific conditions or treatments, and the resulting data are analyzed and compared in order to determine the effects, if any, of these treatments. When an experiment or a series of experiments is introduced in a paper, prior findings are often compared in order to lay the groundwork for the present research; if two or more experiments are presented, their methods will likely be compared in order to point out similarities or differences between subjects, apparatus, materials, or procedures; and in the final discussion, the results are usually compared with previous findings, in order to explain the relevance of the present research. Thus, in the introduction, in the presentation of methods and results, and in the concluding discussion, comparisons are important. Constructions of comparison constitute one of the most crucial and pervasive grammatical and semantic relationships in papers on scientific experiments in psychology.

The most frequent such comparisons can be loosely classified into three categories—those that resemble examples of MODIFICATION, formed through the use of expressions such as *similar to, relative to, identical to, the same as, compared to, compared with, like,* and *unlike;* those that consist of the actual comparative form followed by *than* (*less than, more than, greater than,* etc.); and those that are expressed in statements made with finite forms of the verb *to compare.*

Comparisons with Similar To, The Same As, etc. Like all modifiers (see MODIFICATION), PREDICATIONS, and STATEMENTS, comparisons can be construed as equations of meaning:

> *The procedure in Experiment 2 was similar to Experiment 1.*

> *The procedure in Experiment 2 was identical to Experiment 1.*

These are false equations of meaning, because the word *procedure* cannot be logically or semantically equated with the word *experiment,* unless perhaps by way of metaphor. A procedure is only a part of an experiment; it is not the experiment as a whole. To put this another way, *procedure ≠ Experiment 1.* Correctly written, these sentences might read:

> *The procedure in Experiment 2 was similar to the procedure in Experiment 1.*

> *The procedure in Experiment 2 was identical to the procedure in Experiment 1.*

Now *procedure = procedure.* But the sentences can be more succinct:

> *The procedure in Experiment 2 was similar to that in Experiment 1.*

> *The procedure in Experiment 2 was identical to that in Experiment 1.*

The word *that* now stands for the second use of *procedure,* and the equation of meaning remains correct. Although the foregoing examples may seem unduly simple, all comparisons must be able to stand such a straightforward, logical test.

In general, any two elements of a sentence that are compared should be not only semantically or logically comparable, but also grammatically parallel. Consider the following examples, in which *the same as* has been substituted for *similar to* or *identical to* in the previous sentences:

> *The procedure in Experiment 2 was the same as Experiment 1.*

This is again a false equation of meaning; a procedure, which is only a part of an experiment, cannot logically be compared to an experiment as a whole (*procedure ≠ Experiment 1*).

> *The procedure in Experiment 2 was the same as in Experiment 1.*

This comparison, although perhaps better than the first, is still flawed, because here a noun (*procedure*) is equated with a prepositional phrase (*in Experiment 1*). These elements are not grammatically parallel. There remain the alternatives offered for the use of *similar to* and *identical to* just given:

> *The procedure in Experiment 2 was the same as the procedure in Experiment 1.*
>
> *The procedure in Experiment 2 was the same as that in Experiment 1.*

These comparisons are logically and semantically correct, as well as grammatically parallel; in the latter, more concise, revision, the pronoun *that* again substitutes nicely for the second use of the noun *procedure*.

In the interests of verbal economy, however, the writer should remember that such comparisons or identities may often be expressed without recourse to the phrase *the same as* at all. Instead of the revisions suggested here, one might write, for example, *The procedure was that used in Experiment*

1, or *The procedure from Experiment 1 was used again in Experiment 2.* Both of these statements mean, without any doubt, that the procedure in question was the same procedure in both experiments.

In all of the previous examples, either nouns or nouns and noun substitutes (two instances of the word *procedure;* one instance of the word *procedure* and one instance of the word *that)* are compared. Sometimes, however, comparisons are intended to equate independent clauses:

> *We analyzed these data in the same way as the latency measures.*

There are at least two ways to construe this sentence. One would be to say that the word *way* and the noun phrase *the latency measures* are incorrectly equated by the comparison implied in the adjective *same,* for a way cannot be logically compared with a measure. Given this interpretation, the sentence just presented would be an incorrectly abbreviated form of the following:

> *We analyzed these data in the same way as that in which we analyzed the latency measures.*

Correct although this revision may be, it is verbose. Another interpretation would be that the independent clause *we analyzed this data* has been equated with *the latency measures.* But an independent clause cannot function as a part of speech, so it cannot logically be equated with a noun; to correct the sentence, we need another independent clause instead of the noun. This revision hinges on our taking the phrase *in the same way as* to be a comparative expression that resembles *similar to* or *identical to:*

> *We analyzed these data in the same way as we analyzed the latency measures.*

Now the two independent clauses are properly equated: *We analyzed these data = we analyzed the latency measures.* This, however, is still wordy. Briefer versions might read as follows:

We analyzed these data as we analyzed the latency measures.

We analyzed these data as we did the latency measures.

Again, the use of *same* is not necessary for the comparison to be successful.

The participial phrases *compared to* and *compared with* are often used as a shorthand for comparisons; often in such instances, it is hard to extract the equation of meaning from the sentence:

Visual presentation yielded significant recency effects compared to the controls.

In this sentence, something is being "compared to" the controls, but what? Obviously, it is not the effects. Could it be visual presentation? If so, the comparison is incorrect, because visual presentation and controls are not logically comparable (*visual presentation ≠ controls*). Or is it the fact that visual presentation yielded significant recency effects? If so, the comparison is again incorrect, because an independent clause (*visual presentation yielded significant recency effects*) cannot be equated with a noun (*controls*). In fact, the writer is trying to compare two conditions, one with visual presentation and one that was included as a control. The sentence must therefore be rewritten:

In comparison with the controls, subjects in the visual presentation condition displayed significant recency effects.

When compared with the controls, subjects in the visual presentation condition displayed significant recency effects.

In comparison with the control condition, visual presentation yielded significant recency effects.

When compared with the control condition, visual presentation yielded significant recency effects.

In the first two revisions, the subjects and controls are compared; in the second two, the experimental conditions are compared. Both equations are grammatically and semantically accurate. Note, too, that *compared with* has been substituted for *compared to* in the second and fourth sentences. This is because *compared with* is conventionally held to express differences or contrasts, whereas *compared to* is conventionally thought to express similarity.

In the sentences that follow, just as in the example on visual presentation, an independent clause is followed by either *compared to* or *compared with* plus a noun phrase:

> *The data suggest a gradual development in gap inhibition compared to previous reports.*

> *Most of the subjects were excellent readers when compared with the national reading-level norms.*

Note that in the first sentence, gap inhibition appears to have been equated with previous reports, and that in the second, subjects are equated with norms. Read:

> *The data suggest a gradual development for gap inhibition, in comparison with what has been found previously.*

> *Most of the subjects were excellent readers, whose scores were well above the national reading-level norms.*

Sometimes, comparisons or contrasts can be simpler than the writer seems to think; this is especially the case when a writer chooses the expression *as compared to* or *as compared with*:

> *There were steep trade-offs when attention was divided between two locations as compared to focused on one.*

> *The rate of tip-of-the-tongue states for nonexperimentally learned targets was .14 in Yarmey (1974) as compared with .25 in the present study.*

In the first sentence, *rather than* will do instead:

> *There were steep trade-offs when attention was divided between two locations rather than focused on one.*

In the second sentence, the comparison can be allowed to speak for itself:

> *The rate of tip-of-the-tongue states for nonexperimentally learned targets was .14 in Yarmey (1974); it was .25 in the present study.*

Many problems of comparison can be avoided if one remembers that *compared to* and *compared with*, just as *the same as*, are not always necessary for the expression of comparative meaning. As for *as compared to* and *as compared with*, they are almost always unnecessarily verbose.

Comparisons with *like* or *unlike* resemble those with *similar to*:

> *Unlike the time allotted for reading each script in Experiment 1, there was no time limit in Experiment 2.*

> *Like calcium ingestion, a sex difference was found in sodium ingestion in male and female rats.*

In the first sentence, the noun *time* is ungrammatically contrasted with an independent clause (*there was no time limit*); in the second, *calcium ingestion* is illogically compared to *a sex difference*. Read:

> *In Experiment 1, there was a limit on the time allotted for reading each script; in Experiment 2, there was no time limit.*

> *As with calcium ingestion, a sex difference was found in sodium ingestion in male and female rats.*

A peculiar instance of comparison can occur when one wants to make two comparisons at once, one of which includes the true comparative and the other of which does not:

This procedure will yield scaling coefficients that are as large or larger than those obtained with the standard method.

Changing the context at test affects bias measures as much or more than their associated discrimination measures.

Something can be "as large as" or "larger than," or it can be "as much as" or "more than," but nothing can ever be "as large than" or "as much than"; in both instances, one need only add the word *as* for the two comparative constructions in each sentence to be explicit and complete:

This procedure will yield scaling coefficients that are as large as or larger than those obtained with the standard method.

Changing the context at test affects bias measures as much as or more than their associated discrimination measures.

The Comparative with Than. Constructions of comparison formed with comparative adjectives must likewise be able to stand the test of being pared down to fundamental equations of grammar and meaning. The simplest example would be the following: *A is greater than B.* Here *A* and *B* must be grammatically and semantically comparable: if *A* is an effect, *B* must be an effect; if *A* is a response rate, *B* must be a response rate, and so on. Problems can arise in such comparisons when they are more complicated: *The effect of A is greater than B* is wrong, because an *effect* cannot be compared or equated with *B*; the author means that *The effect of A is greater than the effect of B*, or better still, that *The effect of A is greater than that of B*, but he or she has adopted an illogically abbreviated shorthand instead. The following sentences illustrate these patterns in greater detail:

Incorrect: *Performance in the inverted condition was worse than the other conditions.*

Correct: *Performance in the inverted condition was worse than performance in the other conditions.*

Incorrect: *The distance between the dissimilar pairs was greater than the similar pairs.*

Correct: *The distance between the dissimilar pairs was greater than the distance between the similar pairs.*

The preceding examples consist of predications with the verb *to be* in which the subject is equated with another noun or noun phrase. Another type of predication occurs when the grammatical subject is compared in terms of its attributes, which are usually expressed in prepositional phrases or subordinate clauses following the verb *to be* and the comparative adjective:

Responses were faster following same trials than different trials.

The effect is greater when patterns are presented unilaterally than bilaterally.

In both of these instances, understood clauses are in fact being compared:

Responses were faster following same trials than [than they were following] *different trials.*

The effect is greater when patterns are presented unilaterally than [it is when they are presented] *bilaterally.*

Some writers might object to adding the bracketed material because it would make these sentences longer, but to do so would at least make them semantically clear and grammatically correct. The writer who insists on expressing the same relationships more briefly should remember that, to avoid ambiguity or extreme awkwardness, all of the grammatical elements that follow the comparative adjective should be repeated after *than*:

Responses were faster following same trials than following different trials.

The effect is greater when patterns are presented unilaterally than when they are presented bilaterally.

Another solution would be to substitute *as opposed to* for *than* to link the nouns, or *rather than* for *than* to link the adverbs, in the original sentences:

> *Responses were faster following same trials as opposed to different trials.*

> *The effect is greater when patterns are presented unilaterally rather than bilaterally.*

Other problems in the use of the comparative occur with verbs that constitute statements: *A displayed a greater effect of X than B.* This sentence is confusing because it is hard to tell immediately whether *A* is being compared with *B* or whether *X* is being compared with *B*. To prevent this ambiguity, the writer has various choices, the most likely of which involve the addition of a verb: *A displayed a greater effect of X than B displayed, A displayed a greater effect of X than did B,* or *A displayed a greater effect of X than B did.* In each of these sentences, a clause that was originally deprived of its verb is now explicit, and the ambiguity is resolved.

Note, however, that the second clause in the comparison may remain understood if ambiguity will not result. In the following sentences, which are correct, the bracketed subject and verbs are implied, but they need not be stated:

> *Subjects remember pictures better than* [they remember]*words.*

> *Pictures are remembered better than words* [are]

The following example, however, is ambiguous:

> *Citric acid selectively suppressed fructose more than sucrose.*

Here, it is not clear whether *citric acid suppressed fructose more than it did sucrose,* or whether *citric acid suppressed fructose more than sucrose did.* In the first case, citric acid is suppressing fructose and sucrose; in the second, citric acid and sucrose are suppressing fructose. The proper inclusion of either the subject and verb *it did* or the verb *did* is crucial to the reader's correct understanding of this sentence. In either case, the complete clause must follow *than*. (See also PREDICATION, STATEMENT.)

Comparisons with the Verb To Compare. In formal English prose, the use of the verb *to compare* is straightforward: *A was compared with B; the effect of A was compared with the effect of B; we compared A and B in terms of their effects on X;* and so forth. As with the forms of comparison just discussed, in such sentences, the categories compared must be grammatically and semantically comparable.

> *The performance of the subjects who were given instructions was compared with the subjects who were not.*

Here *performance* under one condition has been falsely equated with the *subjects* under another; corrected, the sentence should read:

> *The performance of the subjects who were given instructions was compared with the performance of the subjects who were not.*

A construction that occurs occasionally in writing on experimental psychology is the infelicitous idiom *to compare for:*

> *Reaction time was compared for letter detection in low-frequency as opposed to high-frequency words.*

Although it is perhaps possible to extract the author's meaning from this sentence, the comparison is nevertheless incomplete. Reaction time, the author tell us, was compared, but the sentence does not actually state what reaction time was compared with. If reaction time of letter detection in low-frequency words was compared with reaction time of letter detection in high-frequency words, the writer should say so.

compose, comprise. Some writers use *compose* and *comprise* interchangeably, but others, who are more careful, distinguish between them. It is correct to say that *wholes comprise their parts*, or that *wholes are composed of their parts*. It is incorrect to say that *wholes are comprised of their parts*, or that *parts comprise wholes*. Although this distinction may seem pedantic, it gives each word a precise meaning, and the meanings are different. If *comprise* and *compose* are used interchangeably, the preferred meaning of *comprise* will simply disappear, and the language will lose a unique, useful expression.

Here are some examples:

Incorrect: *Non-Whites comprised only 11% of the sample.*
Correct: *Non-Whites made up only 11% of the sample.*
Incorrect: *The subject group was comprised of African Americans (12%), Asians (28%), Hispanics (19%), and Whites (41%).*
Correct: *The subject group comprised African Americans (12%), Asians (28%), Hispanics (19%), and Whites (41%).*

In choosing between *compose* and *comprise,* one must keep synonyms in mind, as well as nuances of meaning. The following sentence, for example, is unacceptable on two counts:

The cage floor was comprised of steel rods so that footshock could be easily delivered.

Note, first, that the whole—the floor—cannot be "comprised of" anything; this is incorrect usage. Yet if one were to replace *comprised* with *composed* here, or if one were to delete *was* and *of* so that *comprised* could stand alone, something would still be wrong: it is stylistically pretentious if not semantically peculiar to think of the floor of a rat's cage as *comprising* or as being *composed* of steel rods. The floor is *made* out of the rods, pure and simple. Thus, although the sentences *The cage floor was composed of steel rods so that footshock could be easily delivered* and *The cage floor comprised steel rods so that footshock could be easily delivered* might be semantically correct, the following would be much better:

> *The cage floor was made of steel rods so that footshock could be easily delivered.*

Several possibilities offer themselves to the writer who seeks synonyms for *composed* or *comprised;* examples include *consisted of, contained, included, involved,* and *was made up of.* An experimental design thus does not always have to *comprise* or *be composed of* conditions, although it is fine to say so; it can also *consist of* them. Likewise, an experiment can *include* conditions, because conditions are not all that it *contains;* it can certainly *consist of* or even *involve* certain types of tasks; and it can *comprise* blocks of trials. Studies can *consist of* or be *made up of* several experiments. Neither studies nor experiments, however, USE anything.

comprise. See COMPOSE, COMPRISE.

condition, conditioned. *To condition* is a transitive verb; in the active voice, it always takes an object. If *to condition* is used in the passive voice, the object from the active construction becomes the subject of the verb, and a passive agent is at least implied: The sentence *Rats were conditioned to the target stimulus* is thus the passive form of *I, we, the experimenter,* or *experimenters conditioned the rats to the target stimulus.* Because *to condition* is never an intransitive verb, it is wrong to say that *The rats conditioned to the target stimulus quickly.* It is correct, however, to say that they *were,* or *became,* thus *conditioned.*

consistent with. Although dictionaries are not always to be trusted, all of them seem to agree that *consistent* is an adjective only: *The present results are not consistent with previous findings.* Some scientific writers, however, are inclined to use *consistent with* to introduce an adverbial phrase, or as a transitional expression: *Consistent with pigeon studies of delayed matching to sample (Roitblat & Scopatz, 1983), these two factors had independent effects on performance.*[34] Or again, *Consistent with the previous results, we observed significant impairments.* The problem with these usages is that the adverbial form *consistently* is already available. If one substitutes *consistent* for *consistently*, which is no different from trading INDEPENDENT for *independently* or *liberal* for *liberally*, one thus violates the reader's semantic expectations. If one feels that *consistently* will not do in the examples given here, there are other recourses: *in consistency with*, for example, or *in agreement with*. Or one can rewrite them: *The fact that these two factors had independent effects on performance was consistent with pigeon studies of delayed matching to sample;* and, depending on which nuance the author might prefer, either *We observed significant impairments that were consistent with previous results*, or *The fact that we observed significant impairments was consistent with previous results.* Or one can try still other possibilities: *As we had expected on the basis of previous results, there were significant impairments.* Regardless of the alternative that one chooses, however, the adverbial use of *consistent* is unacceptable. (See also ADVERBS VERSUS ADJECTIVES, COLLINEAR, HIPPOCAMPAL, and INDEPENDENT.)

coordination. The term *coordination* refers primarily to any verbal link created with the conjunctions *and, but, for, nor, or,* or *yet.* Words, phrases, or clauses can be coordinated. A more limited case of coordination involves the "correlative" constructions *both...and, either...or, neither...nor,* and *not only...but also.* Although the rules for coordination can be found in any handbook on English grammar or composition, certain points seem to be particularly interesting with respect to scientific writing.

Standard handbooks nearly always counsel the writer that coordinated verbs governed by a single subject do not need a comma, but that coordinated independent clauses should be separated by a comma. It is noticeable, however, that although scientific writers sometimes do and sometimes do not use the comma, when they do use it they tend to omit the subject of the second coordinated clause. This is probably because the subject of the second clause may often wind up being a pronoun, and scientific writers fear pronouns because they seem imprecise. Here is a typical example:

> *Subjects were presented with a series of statements, and were asked to combine them into a coherent description.*

Most handbooks would suggest that two other versions of this sentence are preferable; the first lacks the comma; the second retains the comma with *and,* followed by the additional subject:

> *Subjects were presented with a series of statements and were asked to combine them into a coherent description.*

> *Subjects were presented with a series of statements, and they were asked to combine them into a coherent description.*

Either revision is acceptable; the difference between them in this instance is a matter of stylistic choice. In the first sentence, the verb *were asked* clearly follows from *subjects,* which is the sentence's grammatical subject; together, *were presented* and *were asked* constitute a *compound verb. Were asked* therefore does not need to be separated from the subject by a comma; indeed a common rule of punctuation tells us that commas ought not to separate subjects and verbs. In the second sentence, the pronoun *they* clearly refers back to *subjects;* this is called a *compound sentence,* because it contains two independent clauses. The writer should not fear ambiguity in either case. (Note, however, that *were* must be repeated in both sentences; if it were not, it would sound as if the subjects, not the experimenters, were doing the asking.)

When coordination is not carried out correctly, mixed grammatical constructions occasionally result, or sometimes sentences will simply be unwieldy because subordination should have been used instead. Here is an example, again with a complete first clause, a comma, and the coordinating conjunction *and* followed by a second verb:

> *The function is shown in Figure 4, and provides a good description of the threshold data.*

In this case, simply adding a new subject (in this case *it*) after *and* will not suffice, because the two halves of the sentence are not grammatically or semantically parallel; one of them should be subordinate to the other. There are two choices:

> *The function, which is shown in Figure 4, provides a good description of the threshold data.*
>
> *The function, which provides a good description of the threshold data, is shown in Figure 4.*

Which of these sentences the writer might prefer depends on context and meaning. The first example is appropriate if emphasis is to be placed on the function as a description of the data; the second is preferable if the main point is simply to let the reader know that the function is shown in Figure 4.

Coordination, then, is not just a grammatical technicality. Certain ideas should be coordinated, others should not. The writer must choose the correct sentence structure, depending on what he or she wishes to say. In general, coordinated elements should be parallel in both content and form (i.e., they must contain logically parallel concepts, expressed in grammatically parallel units of thought). In the original example in the preceding paragraph, much of the initial infelicity derives from the lack of parallelism between the verb forms *is shown* and *provides,* one of which is passive and the other active. Any coordination thus lacking in parallelism will seem awkward to read, even if on some level it makes sense.

The problem of parallelism in coordination can lead to MIXED CONSTRUCTIONS, which read as if two incompatible sentences or portions of sentences have been mistakenly spliced together (subjects and verbs are underlined in the following examples):

> The _cost_ of parts for the interface _is_ low (including chips, board, wire, sockets, and cables) and _takes_ about 8–10 hours to assemble.

> The _clock is derived_ by dividing the computer's master clock and _results_ in a clock speed of 1.20 MHz, close to the maximum speed.

Note that each of these sentences contains a subject and two verbs linked by _and_ (appropriately without the comma). But by the time the writer has arrived at the second verb in each case, he or she has forgotten what the grammatical subject is. In the first case, the cost becomes something that the computer enthusiast is going to have to assemble. In the second, the clock itself is said to "result" in a clock speed. These are errors of STATEMENT. Here are corrected versions:

> The cost of parts for the interface is low (including chips, board, wire, sockets, and cables); one will need about 8–10 hours to assemble it.

> The clock is derived by dividing the computer's master clock; this results in a clock speed of 1.20 MHz, which is close to the maximum.

Coordination also includes the use of conjunctive adverbs or transitional words such as _furthermore, however, indeed, moreover, nevertheless, nonetheless, on the other hand, rather,_ and several others to link independent clauses within the same sentence. In such instances, one does not use a comma with the word of transition, but rather a semicolon. It is remarkable how often writers will ignore this distinction, particularly in the case of _however._ This is not a good mistake to make; to the sensitive reader, it smacks of stylistic and grammatical immaturity. Worse still, it can lead to confusion. If one surrounds a conjunctive adverb with commas, one cannot tell whether it goes with the clause that precedes it or the clause that follows it:

> *Generation effects have been found for recognition of targets studied in related contexts, however, they have not been found for recognition of targets studied in unrelated contexts.*

Here, the semicolon must go either before or after *however*. If it should follow *however*, a contrast would be made with the preceding sentence; if it should go before *however*, the contrast would be made between the two independent clauses in this sentence.

(See under COMMAS, *Commas and coordination: Compound sentences and compound verbs or predicates.* See also AND; BUT; and TRANSITIONAL WORDS AND PHRASES.)

D

dashes. In general, dashes mark shifts of thought within a sentence, or afterthoughts added at the end of a sentence. The shifts of thought are essentially parenthetical, and they usually restate what has just been said in somewhat different terms, often by way of added explanation or specification. The term *afterthought* should not be taken to indicate that the added material is in any way less important than what precedes it. It is simply added on, sometimes in order to append further information or specification with regard to what has just been said; it is usually grammatically parallel with whatever precedes it, but it is not a syntactically inseparable part of the sentence. Here is an example:

> *As an account of the distractor similarity effect, the natural alternative to interference in the perceptual processing is interference— specifically, noise—in the decision process.*[35]

In this sentence, the dashes are necessary because the material that is set off contains a comma; if commas were used, the reader would not know whether *specifically* was more closely tied to *interference* or to *noise*.

> *Massaro (1986, 1988) has also raised questions about the role played by one kind of formal model—connectionism—in psychological theory.[36]*

In this sentence, the dashes are necessary because commas would suggest that *connectionism* stands in apposition to *model*, rather than referring back to the entire phrase that precedes it *(one kind of formal model)*.

> *For each subject, we derived congruity scores—that is, the arithmetical reaction time (RT) difference between sounds having congruent attributes and those having incongruent attributes.[37]*

Here, the dash simply introduces the afterthought at the end of the sentence.

> *In the present article, I present an alternative interpretation of the relationships between formal models and the underlying physical reality—the neural substrate—on the one hand, and the psychological reality—the cognitive processes—on the other.[38]*

This sentence is perhaps unnecessarily complicated; it is usually best not to have more than two dashes within a single sentence, because the repeated shifts of thought can be hard for the reader to follow. On the other hand, in this example the dashes are used correctly.

Note that for shifts of thought within the sentence, commas may sometimes be used for dashes if the shift of thought consists of a word or a phrase; but dashes must always be used within the sentence to set off shifts of thought that consist of clauses. For afterthoughts at the ends of sentences, dashes usually set off words, phrases, or dependent clauses; independent clauses (i.e., sentences) are usually appended to preceding independent clauses (i.e., sentences) by semicolons rather than dashes.

degrees of freedom. Editorial policies regarding F equations and probabilities vary. It is possible to find anthologies of papers with F equations set in a variety of ways, depending on the forms in which the authors have submitted them: degrees of freedom may be introduced with *df* or df, *d.f.* or d.f.; they may be given in parentheses after the F or as subscripts, separated by a comma or by a slash. In APA journals, F equations are set off by commas, $F (1,38) = 25.78$, $p < .01$; in Psychonomic Society journals, brackets are used $[F (1,38) = 25.78, p < .01]$. The writer who intends to submit a paper to a given journal should look at a copy of the journal in advance, ascertain the journal's preferred format for such equations, and type them accordingly. Regardless of the format that one chooses, it is best to be consistent; to mix the styles of the APA and the Psychonomic Society within the same paper, for example, causes problems at all stages of editorial production.

discrimination by. See PERCEPTION BY.

do. Writers should be wary of the slang use of *do*. One does not *do testing*, for example; one *gives* or *takes tests*, or one *conducts* or *carries* them *out*. Nor does one *do training*. On the other hand, one can *do an experiment*, an *analysis*, or even *research*, so it does not pay to be too pedantic about *doing* things either.

dosage, dose. The words *dosage* and *dose* have nearly the same meaning, but not quite. *Dose* refers more to specific individual doses and to their amounts, *dosage* to not only the doses and their amounts but the act of giving them. The following example illustrates both uses:

> On the basis of this data, it seems that xylamidine doses of 1.0 and 2.0 mg/kg would occur at the asymptote of the dose–response curve. Thus, at doses of 1.0 and 2.0 mg/kg, the failure of xylamidine to completely block 5.0-mg/kg peripheral 5-HT-induced anorexia cannot be attributed to an insufficient dosage of xylamidine.[39]

due to. Although *due to* as a prepositional construction introducing an adverbial phrase is perhaps sanctioned by contemporary usage, many writers still think it peculiar jargon to be avoided:

> *The Zöllner illusion and related effects possibly occur due to lateral neural interactions.*[40]

A more rigorous stylistic convention would recommend the use of *because of* instead of *due to* here; an effect may *be due to* something, but the effect *occurs because of* it. If one insists on *due to* in this sentence, one should write:

> *The Zöllner illusion and related effects are possibly due to lateral neural interactions.*

Otherwise, one would choose:

> *The Zöllner illusion and related effects occur possibly because of lateral neural interactions.*

The proper use of *due to* thus completes predications either expressed or implied: *effects* due to something are *effects that are* due to something. When the subject and verb constitute a statement rather than a predication, either *because of* or *owing to* should be used. Both of the following sentences are correct:

> *The downward shift in attending was due to the subjects' inability to discern the event's intrinsic organization.*

> *Attending shifted downward, owing to the subjects' inability to discern the event's intrinsic organization.*

Finally, note the difference between *due* and *due to*. Thanks are *due* people who help run an experiment. It is highly unlikely that the experimenter's thanks would be *due to* them, unless they had vigorously admonished the experimenter to thank them.

E

each. The word *each* is always singular; it always refers to *each one* of two or more items. Thus it makes no sense to write that *there was an interval of 30 sec between each trial*, because the phrase *each trial* refers to only one trial and an interval cannot occur between only one trial. Alternatives include *the intertrial interval was 30 sec, the interval between trials was 30 sec*, or *there were intervals of 30 sec between trials*. Likewise, one cannot logically say that *an interval of 5 sec separated each trial;* instead, *intervals of 5 sec (5-sec intervals) separated the trials*.

each vs. a, an, or the. Occasionally, in the attempt to explain what happened in each individual session, trial, or condition in an experiment, a writer will attempt to employ the indefinite article: *During an experimental session, stimuli were presented on line…* Such expressions are ambiguous, for they lead the reader to ask the question, "*Which* experimental session? *Any* of them? Only one *specific* session? *All* of the sessions?" A better alternative would be to write, *During each experimental session, stimuli were presented on line…;* here the reader does not need to pause to figure out when the stimuli were presented. Likewise, if a writer declares that *An experimental session was approximately 30 min long*, the reader can only ask, "Which one?" Again, *each* is the solution: *Each experimental session was approximately 30 min long.*

The same reasoning applies to subjects: *During testing, a subject wore a mask that limited his or her vision.* Which subject? A subject in this experiment? A subject who just happened to be in the room at the time? Only one of the several subjects in this experiment? One alternative would be to write, *During testing, the subject wore a mask that limited his or her vision.* In this case, *the subject* stands for "the subjects in the experiment," which will often suffice. Sometimes, however, even *the subject* can seem to imply that only one subject is under consideration. With *each,* on the other hand, no ambiguity can occur: *During testing, each subject wore a mask that limited his or her vision.* In this way, the reader knows that "the subjects" are being referred to, but the writer does not have to resort to the plural in order to say so.

easily vs. easy to. It is better to write of *tasks that are easy to perform,* or of *targets that are easy to detect,* than it is to write of *tasks that are easily performed* or *targets that are easily detected.* This is because the present tense of *to be* followed by *easy to* with the infinitive denotes a potential action, which is what the writer wishes to express. *Easily* with the past participle cannot adequately denote a potential action when it follows *to be* in the present tense, because this construction suggests a fixed state (consider, by way of analogy, the statement *this effect is well documented*). With the past tense or with the auxiliary *can,* however, *easily* works well: *The tasks were easily performed* (or *the tasks were performed easily*) refers to a past completed action; *the tasks can be easily performed* (or *the tasks can be performed easily*) refers to a potential one. But to say that *the tasks are easily performed* conflates the connotation of potential action and present state, thereby causing an ambiguity that requires one to read the sentence more than once. Another word that leads to similar problems in the idiom of contemporary experimental psychologists is *readily,* which in the scientific context sounds rather odd. If *readily* actually means *easily,* it should readily be avoided. A final reason for preferring *easy to* plus the infinitive instead of *easily* plus the past participle is that the former is concrete and direct, whereas the latter is stylistically loose and flabby. Whenever possible, one should always at least consider the use of infinitives instead of participles. (See also PASSIVE VOICE.)

effects and interactions. Statistical effects are the mathematically calculated effects of variables; statistical interactions occur when the effect of one variable affects, or interacts with, the effect of another variable. Therefore, in analyzing experimental data, one refers to *effects* and *interactions*. There are many ways to do this; the most straightforward read more or less like this:

> *The main effect of location was significant...The main effect of noise type was also significant...Pairwise comparisons revealed that the no-noise and compatible-noise conditions did not differ, while all other differences were significant...The interaction of noise type and location was also significant.*[41]

The effects and interaction are discussed separately; it would be redundant to refer to the interaction itself as a significant "interaction effect."

Another way of labeling an interaction is to use a multiplication sign: *the waveform × displacement interaction* thus substitutes for *the interaction between waveform and displacement* or *the interaction of waveform and displacement.* Any of these versions is acceptable, although some writers admittedly do not like to use the multiplication sign for this purpose. The writer who writes of *the interaction of waveform by displacement,* however, is likely to discover that editors may prefer the multiplication sign to this use of *by.* There seems to be no consistent rationale for this choice; it owes largely to the conventions followed by particular journals.

either...or.... The correlative construction *either...or*, like *neither...nor,* provides a means of coordinating two, and only two, alternatives:

> *The subjects were either students or other volunteers from the university community.*

> *The subjects were graduate students, staff members, or faculty members.*

In the first example, there are two alternatives; in the second, there are more than two, so *either* is not used.

The constructions that follow *either...or...* must be grammatically parallel.

Incorrect: *The characters were to either be on the left or the right.*
Incorrect: *The characters were to be either on the left or the right.*
Incorrect: *The characters were to be on either the left or right.*
Correct but wordy: *The characters were to be either on the left or on the right.*
Correct and less wordy: *The characters were to be on either the left or the right.*
Correct, still less wordy: *The characters were to be on the left or the right.*
Correct and least wordy: *The characters were to be on the left or right.*

As is often the case in scientific writing, hyperprecision is not necessary; here, *either* is ultimately superfluous.
(See also PARALLELISM.)

e.g. *E.g.* is the abbreviation for the Latin *exempli gratia* (English "for example"). Probably no abbreviation is less well understood. *E.g.* does not mean "see," "that is" ("i.e."), or "compare" ("cf."). And since it literally means "for example," it must refer to an antecedent nominal construction. Thus, in the sentence *Many researchers (e.g., Averbach & Coriell, 1961; Chow, 1985; Coriell, 1961; Treisman, Russell, & Green, 1975) have replicated this effect, e.g.* is used correctly, for the names that follow exemplify the researchers who have just been alluded to as a general category. But to write, *This effect has been replicated frequently (e.g., Averbach & Coriell, 1961; Chow, 1985; Coriell, 1961; Treisman, Russell, & Green, 1975)*, is jarringly incorrect, because the names do not exemplify anything that has actually been named before the parentheses.

In the latter instance, two solutions are possible. The first, and more common, sounds unwieldy but is at least correct: *This effect has been replicated frequently (see, e.g., Averbach &*

Coriell, 1961; Chow, 1985; Coriell, 1961; Treisman, Russell, & Green, 1975). That is, the reader is being told to look at the works cited, so that he or she may find examples of the effect's having been replicated. The second is precise and highly to be recommended, but it is rarely attempted, because it requires that the writer pay careful attention to the grammatical relation between the items inside and outside the parentheses: *This effect has been replicated frequently (e.g., by Averbach & Coriell, 1961; Chow, 1985; Coriell, 1961; Treisman, Russell, & Green, 1975).* That is, at the end of the sentence the reader silently asks "By whom?"—and the author replies with *e.g.,* the answering preposition *by,* and the names in question. (See also ABBREVIATIONS, LATIN.)

example. The word *example* is properly a noun, not an adjective. It is therefore correct to write, *Examples of easy pairs include...* But it is incorrect to write, *Example easy pairs include...* There is no reason to use nouns as adjectives when other, more conventional means of modification are available.

exclamation marks. Exclamation marks conclude emotional utterances or commands; they are rarely used in formal essayistic prose, other than for the unusual stylistic effect. Although exclamations may in retrospect be appropriate for the popularized recounting of strikingly important scientific discoveries, they are far removed from the writing that is done to record the methodical processes of scientific experimentation. Scientific writing consists of the straightforward presentation of problems, clear descriptions of methods, careful and detailed reports of results and analyses, and temperate, well-reasoned discussions of implications. In such a rhetorical context, exclamations are seldom appropriate.

experiment, experiments. Although it may sometimes

seem unnecessary to do so, in a paper with more than one experiment it is always best to refer to the experiments with their numerical appelations: *Experiment 1, Experiment 2, Experiment 3,* and so forth. These experiments may together be called *the present experiments.* One should therefore use the phrase *the present experiment,* in the singular, when only one experiment is reported in a paper. If in the middle of a section on Experiment 3, for example, one should refer to *the present experiment,* the reader will probably hesitate, wondering whether this term really does signify Experiment 3 alone, or whether all of the present experiments mentioned in the paper are in fact meant.

The same ambiguity that sometimes afflicts the present experiment can accompany the phrase this experiment, which one would do well to avoid. In like manner, some writers choose to refer to the current experiment, but in the present author's view, this is even less preferable. The word current suggests that the experiment might still be under way; the word present will more likely be construed to signify what is presently being discussed.

As for the word study, one should use it with care. One carries out, performs, or simply does an experiment or a series of experiments in order to study a particular problem. The experiment or experiments constitute a *study.* But when one writes a report about the experiments, one is also writing a *study* of them. Therefore, it is probably safest to reserve the phrase *the present study* for referring to the present article in which one is discussing an experiment or experiments, and not to the study that one has carried out. Otherwise, the reader will be unable to tell whether *the present study* refers to Experiment 1, 2, or 3, to all three experiments together, or to the report of these experiments that is being read at present.

experiments, personification of. See PERSONIFICATION; see also PASSIVE VOICE.

F

find, found. *Scientists*—that is, researchers, experimenters, investigators, or others—*find* results by studying and analyzing the data that they obtain or gather in their experiments. *Experiments,* however, do not find anything, because experiments are not animate beings. Studies, research, analyses of variance, or results themselves cannot find anything either; always the researcher performs, carries out, or does studies, research, or analysis in order to obtain findings. To say that an experiment can find something is to err in making a STATEMENT; the illogical statement thus made is an unnecessary and inappropriate mode of PERSONIFICATION.

findings by, from, in, and of. Paintings are by painters, books are by authors, reports are by writers; this is because painters, authors, or writers create what they paint or write. Experimental findings, however, are not *findings by experimenters;* they are instead the *findings of experimenters,* or they are the *experimenters' findings.* Retrospectively, one may say that findings come *from* particular experiments or one can refer to them as the findings *in* those experiments. They are not the findings *of* experiments, because this would suggest that the experiments found the findings, which is impossible. Findings can also be called the *results of* experiments. But findings are not works of art, so they can never be by anybody.

following. Most scientific writers seem to prefer the word *following* instead of *after* when they refer to sequences of events, perhaps because *following* can seem to connote *immediately after* and can therefore seem more precise. Yet the word *after* is not at all vague. If a person goes to the store and goes home after that, the one action clearly follows the other. If subjects are debriefed after a test, they are debriefed following it. The difference between *after* and *following* in such instances is that the former is short and the latter long, a fact that in itself ought to recommend the use of *after*.

Indeed the use of *following* often goes hand in hand with unnecessary jargon and abstraction:

> *Following completion of the questionnaire, the subjects received the instructions for the test.*

Note that although the phrase *following completion* consists of only two words, *completion* is an abstract noun, and the sentence does not in fact state who completed the questionnaire; literally, it could have been anybody. Here are three alternatives:

> *After they had completed the questionnaire, the subjects received the instructions for the test.*

> *After having completed the questionnaire, the subjects received the instructions for the test.*

> *After they had answered the questions, the subjects received the instructions for the test.*

The reader should not be deceived by the greater number of words in each of these revisions; more words, if used correctly, often confer greater accuracy and precision of meaning. In each instance, the reader is told who answered the questions, and the act of answering them is expressed by a concrete verb (*had completed, having completed, had answered*) rather than the abstract noun *completion.* Thus, the use of *after* is to be recommended. It is not merely shorter and simpler than *following,* it does not sound as pretentious. It can help the writer avoid unnecessary jargon. (See also PRIOR TO.)

for example. *For example* is a transitional prepositional phrase; it functions after the manner of transitional conjunctive adverbs such as *however* or *nevertheless: Researchers have shown, for example, that explicit and implicit memory are affected* *by modality shifts between study and test.* In this sentence, the modality shifts are an example of a more general principle, and *for example* makes that relationship clear. In this way, *for example* is used to link sentences. *For example* is not, however, a substitute for *such as* or *like.* It is thus wrong to write that *certain drugs, for example naltrexone and serotonin, affect alcoholics' consumption of alcoholic beverages.* Correctly written, this sentence should read, *Certain drugs, such as naltrexone and serotonin, affect alcoholics' consumption of alcoholic beverages.* If the writer nevertheless wishes to retain *for example,* he or she must indicate that it represents a shift of thought: *Certain drugs (e.g., naltrexone and serotonin) affect alcoholics' consumption of alcoholic beverages; certain drugs—for example, naltrexone and serotonin—affect alcoholics' consumption of alcoholic beverages.* Of these two alternatives, the parenthetical construction with *e.g.* is better, because it is less verbose. Whenever *for example* introduces one or more examples, *such as* is likely to be an appropriate alternative.

further vs. furthermore. *Further* is either an adverb or an adjective, denoting distance in a figurative sense. Thus, it differs from farther, which is more concrete: They walked farther, but they spoke further. Although the OED counsels that further may be a conjunctive adverb for making transitions of argument from sentence to sentence, in contemporary American usage further sounds peculiar in the initial position, as in the following example: Further, this problem is not our major concern. In such cases, if one is indeed developing an argument, one should use furthermore. If, in the face of the OED, one requires a good reason to justify this, one need only remember that furthermore clearly conveys the personal voice of the writer, whereas further does not. In the following sentence, if *further* were used, its proximity to *across* would surely at first mislead the reader into thinking of physical distance rather than the author's argument.

Furthermore, across the compression conditions, there were increas-

ingly negative slopes....[42]

Often, however, an argument is not at all what the writer has in mind: In listing a series of instructions given to subjects, for example, it would be incorrect to write, *The subjects were told that the same letters would appear on every trial. Further, subjects were told that the location of the letters would vary from trial to trial.* Here the writer confuses the reader, who will at first read *further* to mean *furthermore*, even though that is not what the writer means. In this case, either *further* should follow the verb *told* —*Subjects were further told that...*—or one should substitute *in addition* or *also*, thus: *Subjects were told in addition [Subjects were also told] that the location of the letters would vary from trial to trial.* The following sentences illustrate the sequential implication of *further* well:

> *In summary, these data confirm and further illustrate the adverse sampling characteristics of ML estimation with 2AFC data. The data suggest, further, that the Bayesian method is almost devoid of these adverse sampling characteristics.*[43]

G

generality, generalize. A *general effect* is an effect that applies to or has been found throughout a whole or in all the members of a group, or that is prevalent within the whole or among the members of the group. A *general description*, however, is merely approximate, and a *general answer* is indefinite and likely to be vague or inadequate. *Generality* is the quality or state of being general, and its meanings similarly vary.

One concept of generality is important in all fields of science. In scientific experiments, specific effects are found under specific conditions. A goal of the scientist, once an effect has been found, is to determine whether or not the effect can be found under other specific conditions as well. If it is thus found, the effect can loosely be said to possess *generality*, because it now appears to occur more generally—that is, within a wider range of circumstances—than it did before. If the effect cannot be found under other conditions, it is limited in its generality. The effect's occurring under additional circumstances can also be termed *generalizing*. The effect has either *generalized* or *been generalized*, again because it is found over a wider range of conditions than was originally the case.

The terms *generality* and *generalize* can be difficult to use, partly because of the range of their meanings. To refer to the "generality" of a computer software package, for example, as in the sentence *Our purpose was to evaluate the generality of MEL*, is to say almost nothing. Does this reviewer intend to consider the general applicability of MEL for classroom use, to evaluate MEL as a tool for researchers, or to consider MEL's general usefulness in all respects? If, for example, the reviewer wishes to determine the general utility of MEL for the presentation of experimental paradigms to students, he or she should say so directly.

The verb *generalize* raises other problems. One cannot attempt to discover, for example, whether or not *the results of Experiment 1 would generalize to new subjects and a different instrument of measurement*, because this implies that a result can actually *become* a subject or an instrument of measurement. The point here is really whether or not results similar to those already found might be obtained in a second experiment with new subjects taking a test different from the one taken before. In like manner, the *procedure in Experiment 1* cannot *generalize to Experiment 2*, because a procedure cannot become an experiment; and *performance* can never *generalize to other conditions*, because performance cannot become an experimental condition. Procedures can, however, be generally applied in more than one experiment, and performance in one condition can generalize to performance in another. The same problem arises in the discussion of effects:

It was expected that the effects of orientation would generalize to the tilted array.[44]

Here we are told that *effects* could become an *array*, which is impossible; the author seems to mean that these perceptual effects will generalize to be found also in the perception of other kinds of shapes. When something generalizes, it is extended to cover a greater portion of experience, but it does not actually become anything else.

gerunds. See -ING WORDS.

gestalt, Gestalt. In German, nouns always take the initial uppercase letter: *Gestalt*. In English, however, *Gestalt* takes the initial uppercase letter only if it refers to the Gestalt school of psychology or to the Gestalt psychologists who belonged to it or who may be considered their descendants; otherwise, when the word simply refers to a configuration or formal pattern of psychological phenomena, it should be written in lowercase: *gestalt*.

H

hands-on. The notion of *hands-on experience* or *hands-on training*, as opposed to mere *experience* or *training*, has taken hold in colloquial and pseudoprofessional uses of English since the 1960s. It suggests origins within a modern sense of alienation. Implicit in the idea of doing things with one's "hands on" is the assumption that throughout history until now, all learning and education have somehow been passive activities, involving audiences who simply sat and read books or listened to lecturers, without ever really participating in the acquisition of knowledge. "Hands-on" learning, on the other hand, implies that one is somehow actively engaged: One does not just read about experiments that have been performed, for example; one performs—or re-per-forms—them, preferably with one's hands on a computer keyboard. Never mind that previously the idea of "hands-on" participation was simply taken for granted when it was deemed necessary; today, it must be thus named, as if we need to convince ourselves that in acting with our hands on we are more advanced or enlightened than our historical predecessors. The term also introduces an unnecessary specification of facts that are in themselves straightforward and simple. Anyone who would learn how to drive a car must at some point get behind the wheel; why, then, refer to this as "hands-on" driver's education? Likewise, it is clear that students in experimental psychology, chemistry, or physics at some point will have to do laboratory work if they are to learn their respective subject matters thoroughly, just as they have always had to do; why bother, then, to call such activity "hands-on" at all?

having. *Having* is the present participle or the gerund of the verb *to have*. There is little reason, however, for the participial form *having* to function as a preposition. Thus *a circle having a radius of 3° visual angle* is really a *circle with a radius of 3° visual angle, stimuli having different perceptual properties* are *stimuli with different perceptual properties,* and *subjects having musical training* are *subjects with musical training* or *subjects who have [had] musical training.* The prepositional use of *having* exemplifies a more general tendency whereby present participles are allowed to stand for prepositions, presumably because this enables the writer to avoid knowing which preposition to choose. (The most ubiquitous instance of this practice is exemplified by the vogue for the participle USING.)

high-frequency, low-frequency. These terms take hyphens when used as adjectives. This rule applies regardless of what type of frequency they refer to: *high-frequency tones* (tones of high frequency), *high-frequency words* (words that occur frequently). In their comparative forms, however, they do not take hyphens: *higher frequency tones, higher frequency words*. (See HYPHENATED TERMS.)

hippocampal. *Hippocampal* is an adjective derived from the noun *hippocampus*. At times the hippocampus can be damaged, or, in the interests of scientific experimentation, hippocampal damage can be inflicted on the rat as a means of studying the effects of particular experimental manipulations on memory or learning. Such rats, which have *hippocampal lesions*, are *hippocampally damaged*, not *hippocampal damaged* or *hippocampal-damaged;* this is because the adjective *hippocampal* is not an adverb in English. This usage is part of the more general trend in scientific writing whereby writers sometimes let adjectives take on the adverbial function: thus COLLINEAR replaces *collinearly*, CONSISTENT replaces *consistently*, INDEPENDENT replaces *independently*, and so forth. When the only difference between such words is the addition of the suffix *-ly*, it is hard to see why that suffix should not be used. (See also ADVERBS VERSUS ADJECTIVES.)

hyphenated terms. Hyphenation can be difficult, if only because of the various policies of journals, editors, and writers. A glance at almost any current issue of the leading psychology journals will reveal considerable variety in hyphenation, even within single articles.[45] If one is familiar with a given journal or series of journals, one can attempt to gain an insight into policies regarding hyphenation simply by scanning a few articles in order to discover whether any preferred forms do exist. If this does not seem to help, a good dictionary, along with *The Chicago Manual of Style,* will be the best help. Yet some editors and writers will differ with the dictionaries, and many hyphenated and nonhyphenated compounds are too new to have found their way into any dictionary yet. The following few guidelines may be of some help:

Hyphenated Adjectives
1. As a rule, any compound adjective takes the hyphen if

the compound begins with either a word designating a numeral or the numeral itself, or if it begins with the words *high*
or *low*, *long* or *short*, or *left* or *right*.

> *one-way analysis*
> *second-order equation*
> *two-dimensional object*
> *three-dimensional perception*
> *high-frequency word*
> *low-frequency tones*
> *long-term effects*
> *short-term effects*
> *left-handed subjects*
> *right-handed subjects*

This rule holds regardless of the position of the compound
adjective in the sentence, although in some of the instances
above, other alternatives are preferable if the compound
adjective does not precede the noun:

> *The objects were three-dimensional.*
> *The subjects were right-handed.*

But:

> *The tones were high in frequency.*
> *a magnitude of the first order*

2. Although compound adjectives such as *high-frequency*
and *low-frequency* take the hyphen, one should drop this
hyphen when other words are combined with them to make
still longer adjectival phrases:

> *high-frequency tone*, but *high spatial frequency grating*
> *low-frequency word*, but *low temporal frequency condition*

3. Comparative or superlative forms of such compound

adjectives need not take a hyphen:

lower frequency tones
higher order effects
lowest frequency conditions

If, however, ambiguity might result, the hyphen should be retained:

The best-informed student.

4. When phrases such as those in (1) are noun phrases rather than compound adjectives, the hyphen is unnecessary:

long-term effects; effects over the long term
high-frequency tones; tones with a high frequency

5. Other compound adjectives consisting of an adjective followed by a noun need not be hyphenated, unless ambiguity will result:

lexical decision task
passive avoidance task
repeated measures ANOVA
large-brained mammals
single-target condition

In the fourth example, the hyphen is necessary to show that the mammals have large brains; otherwise the reader might comically infer that the mammals are large, with brains. In the fifth example, the hyphen signifies that the condition has a single target; otherwise, the reader might momentarily infer that there was a single condition, with a target.

6. Compound adjectives that consist of nouns followed by adjectives take the hyphen when they precede the noun that

they modify:

context-dependent effect
drug-induced amnesia
error-prone subjects

Note that such constructions often consist of the noun followed by the past participle (as in the second example). When such forms follow the noun, hyphens are usually optional or unnecessary:

*a humidity-controlled chamber; the chamber was humidity con-
trolled*

7. Compound adjectives that consist of two nouns need not take the hyphen unless ambiguity will result:

stimulus onset asynchrony
signal detection theory

Yet another rule of thumb here is that there is usually no need to hyphenate such phrases when they are commonly used and understood within the profession:

reaction time measurements

8. Adverbs that end in *-ly* need never be hyphenated to other words, because the ending ensures that the adverb's semantic role cannot be mistaken:

horizontally symmetrical shapes
prenatally stressed males

An adverb that does not end in *-ly* and that combines with a present participle to modify a noun that follows should be hyphenated:

long-lasting effects
best-fitting solution

An adverb that does not end in *-ly* and that combines with an adjective or a past participle to modify a noun that follows should be hyphenated:

the above-mentioned experiment; the experiment mentioned above
a well-run class; the class was well run

If an adverb modifies an ensuing adverb that is itself part of a compound adjective before a noun, no hyphen is necessary:

a very well equipped laboratory

9. In general, many compound adjectives that consist of a preposition plus a noun are so new that they contain hyphens; as they are assimilated into the language, the hyphens may or may not drop out:

follow-up
in-line
off-line
on-line
on-screen
warm-up

The best policy here is simply to include the hyphen if one is unsure.

Note, however, that when such phrases do not precede the noun, they are usually nominal or adverbial. In this position, when they act as noun phrases, they retain the hyphen:

a follow-up
a warm-up

—but when they are adverbial phrases, they do not:

responses were recorded on line
the images were viewed on screen

Hyphenated Versus Nonhyphenated Nouns and Noun Phrases
Compound nouns can be fused, hyphenated, or written separately without hyphens. These choices should be made in accordance with whatever dictionary one prefers, or with whatever dictionary a given journal recommends. At times, however, a journal will differ with the dictionary, preferring *tradeoff* to *trade-off,* for example; and often the terms that the scientific writer is most concerned about will be too technical or too new for any dictionary to include them. In this case, one should follow one's intuition as best one can. Here is a miscellaneous list of several compound nouns, in which all three types occur:

airpuff
airstream
armrest
bandwidth
barpress
beam splitter
body weight
brainstem
by-product
buttonpress
cathode-ray tube
chinrest; chin- and headrest
chi-square
C language
crossover
cuelight
cutoff frequency
database
disk buffer

disk drive
E-maze
endpoint
exposure box
fade-out
feeding box
firmware
follow-up
food cup
footshock
goalbox
goal cage
goal cup
Grice box
half-field
hard disk
hardware
headrest; head- and chinrest
headspace
houselight
keylight
keypeck
keypress
left-key peck
leverpress
long-box
lookup
matching-to-position
matching-to-sample
nose poke
pin prick
pushbutton
P-maze
right-key peck
screen buffer
setup
shuttlebox

sidewall
Skinner box
sniffstrip
space bar
stainless steel
startbox
start door
startup disk
tailpinch
tape recorder
test box
T-maze
tone discrimination
trade-off, tradeoff
treadlepress
t test
videocassette
video recorder
videotape
voice key
warm-up (adj., n.)
x-, y-, z-axis
x-, y-, z- coordinate
x, y, z dimension

Hyphenation of Prefixes

In general, prefixes need not be hyphenated unless ambiguity of meaning or pronunciation will result. (Note that this rule differs from the common practice in much nonscientific writing.)

co-occur
co-worker
intertrial
intra-item
preexisting
recreation

re-creation
remove
re-move

For hyphenation of units of measurement, see ABBREVIA-
TIONS OF MEASUREMENT.

I

identical to. See COMPARISON.

i.e. This abbreviation stands for the Latin *id est,* which means "that is." The abbreviation is used within parentheses; outside the parentheses, it should be spelled out in its English translation. It should not be confused with *e.g.,* which means "for example." (See also ABBREVIATIONS, LATIN; and E.G.)

if...then. When *if* introduces an adverbial clause of condition, which is joined with a main clause that gives the result of that condition, we have a conditional sentence. Often—although not always—the *if* clause comes first. In such instances, many writers feel compelled to add *then* at the beginning of the main clause. This use of *then* is not necessarily wrong, although it is often superfluous. Sometimes, however, it can be very helpful.

A good rule might be the following: In general, do not use *then* to introduce the main clause, unless the reader clearly needs a signal that the main clause is about to begin. This principle is based on the common rule of thumb that the addition of *then* at the start of the main clause tends to lessen the emphasis on what follows. Any notion that *if...then* is somehow inherently appropriate to scientific writing ought therefore to be dispensed with at once.

In the following sentence, *then* would be unnecessary:

If there is some small effect of this manipulation, it would serve to diminish the influence of abrupt onset in Experiment 1.[46]

Note that here *it* refers back to the effective subject of the preceding *if* clause (*effect*); commonly, if the main clause and the preceding *if* clause have the same subject, or if the main clause begins with a pronoun that refers back to the subject of the main clause, the word *then* will not be needed to introduce the main clause.

In this sentence too, *then* would be unnecessary:

If this were the case, it would provide additional support for the generalization that the effects of structural variables are modulated by frequency; it would also address whether the naming of a word necessarily requires decomposition into syllabic components.[47]

Note that this second example resembles the first; but this time, the pronoun *it* constitutes a "broad" reference; it refers to the meaning of the entire *if* clause, rather than to that clause's grammatical subject. In such instances, again with the pronoun referring back to what precedes it, *then* is likely to be superfluous. The pronoun *it* provides an adequate signal that the main clause is underway.

Note that the greater complexity of a sentence does not necessarily mean that *then* is necessary either:

If a person's eyes were to be totally immobilized mechanically, pharmacologically, or by virtue of clinical pathology, each intended change of gaze should alter his or her perceived direction of gaze in a stepwise fashion so that a static visual scene imaged upon his or her immobile retina would appear to be egocentrically displaced.[48]

In this complex sentence, the close of the initial series of three elements is signaled by the word *or,* and the subject that begins with the word *each* cannot possibly be misconstrued. The inclusion of *then* would only provide a stumbling block for the reader.

In the following two examples, the authors clearly thought

that *then* was of use:

> *If the influence of processing level on frequency judgments im-*
> *plicates an indirect model, then an examination of the nature of the*
> *indirect coding is warranted.*[49]

> *If response bias were known to be a significant factor in the recog-*
> *nition process, then a model of response selection that correctly*
> *incorporates response bias would be desirable.*[50]

Note, however, that *then* could just as well be removed with
no change of meaning; the stylistic effect would be more
emphatic and concise; the writers would sound as if they had
greater confidence in their assertions:

> *If the influence of processing level on frequency judgments im-*
> *plicates an indirect model, an examination of the nature of the*
> *indirect coding is warranted.*

> *If response bias were known to be a significant factor in the recog-*
> *nition process, a model of response selection that correctly incorpo-*
> *rates response bias would be desirable.*

When is it correct to add *then* at all? The following sentence
gives an excellent example:

> *If distance is in fact crucial in our task, then by varying stimulus*
> *eccentricity, and thus interelement distance, we should modulate*
> *the extent to which foils influence performance.*[51]

Here the participial phrase (*by varying stimulus eccentricity,*
and thus interelement distance) intervenes between the *if* clause
and the main clause; because the participial phrase belongs
with that which follows rather than precedes it, *then* provides
a clear signal of that fact. Without *then*, the reader might
wonder whether the participial phrase were in fact a dangling modifier accompanying the noun *distance*. With *then*,
the reader cannot make this mistake and is thus prepared for
the main clause well in advance.

   In summary: Use *then* to introduce the main clause only if

ambiguity might result from its absence.

imagery. Outside the world of experimental psychology, *imagery* is a collective noun that refers to the presence of images, as, for example, in written, and particularly literary, discourse, or in discussion of the fine arts. In experimental psychology, however, the question arises of how to verbalize the mental process of generating and making use of images, for the word *imagery* does not conventionally connote any action. Indeed there is in modern English no good verb for the act of forming images in the mind, and there is no noun that describes this act in the way that the psychologist might like. *Imagination* is far too general and fraught with metaphysical baggage, as is the verb *to imagine*, and *to image* is probably too specific. If I *image* something, I am simply forming a particular image in my mind; and although the gerund *imaging* could be used to refer to the making of images in general, whether as an ability, a capacity, or simply a process, this would still seem to connote the actual making of an image more than a facility for doing so. In ordinary prose, one therefore simply refers to the ability to create images or to think in them, and no one has ever found it necessary to coin a word such as *eidopoesis* to label this activity.

The psychologists' solution to this dilemma is, from the lay person's perspective, peculiar: the noun *imagery* is no longer conceived to stand for the product or products of a mental process but rather for the process itself. A person who can think in images with ease is thus called *a high imager;* such a person is said to have *high imagery ability*. Subjects are grouped into *imagery conditions*, for which they receive *imagery instructions*. These are strange, unconventional locutions. Although it is true that more conventional and less jarring alternatives may require more words, in the interests of semantic precision a few extra words should be preferable to *imagery ability*. A *high imager* could thus become a person with an appreciable ability to think in images or create them. A person's *imagery ability* could simply be his or her ability or capacity to create or think in images. The noun *imagery* does not make a very good adjective; if it is possible to do without this usage, one should attempt it.

impact. *Impact* is a noun, not a verb. It is incorrect to say that one thing *impacts* on another; it is correct to say that something *has an impact* on another thing, or that something strikes another thing *with a certain impact.* In contemporary usage, the verb *impact* is usually unnecessary jargon substituted for the verb *affect,* just as the noun *impact* is usually jargon for the noun *effect.* Unless one is discussing measurable physical relationships, *impact* is almost always a bombastic word that should be avoided.

imperatives or infinitives as modifiers. The heading for this entry may seem ambiguous, but this is because the material to which it refers is unclear. It stands for the practice of letting what appears to be the imperative form of the verb, or perhaps the infinitive form of the verb without the preposition *to,* stand as an adjectival modifier before the noun. Examples would be phrases such as *the copy condition, the generate condition, rehearse instructions, the rehearse condition,* or *remember or forget cues.* From the point of view of standard English grammar and generally accepted conventions of style, these locutions are not only peculiar and infelicitous, they are wildly incorrect.

The origins of such expressions are unclear. Perhaps because the instructions given to subjects seem to provide a simple means of characterizing experimental conditions, the imperative form with which the instructions are actually given comes to be thought of as a name. Thus, because subjects are told in direct discourse to "rehearse" material before being tested for their memory of it, these subjects become the subjects in the *rehearse* condition. Yet although this reasoning would account for *rehearse conditions* or *instructions,* it cannot account for the similar naming of types of behavior, as in the peculiar phrase *a jump activity*, nor can it explain a title such as the following: *Flexible coding of temporal information by pigeons: Event durations as remember and forget cues for temporal samples.*[52] Pigeons and other non-human subjects, after all, are not verbally instructed to re-hearse, remember, or forget. One is therefore led to conclude either that the imperative form has been generalized to apply to cases in which instructions are only indirectly or implicitly present because the experiment involves animal learning, or that such constructions actually represent the infinitive at work, on the analogy between infinitives and nouns, with the infinitive substituting for the noun as an adjectival modifier. Because *to remember* and *to forget* are infinitives, and because infinitives can function as nouns (*To exercise is healthy*), per-haps the infinitive is being used in place of an adjective. As for the egregious phrase *jump activity*, here this principle has been applied to the description of observed behavior of any kind, not just learning. It is to be hoped that such verbal devices are not destined to become commonplace in written English.

In many such instances, a simple adjective will work better than the imperative form; whenever such an adjective is available, it should be chosen. Therefore, instead of *rehearse instructions*, write *rehearsal instructions*; for *rehearse condition*, one should write *rehearsal condition*. For the redundant jargon illustrated in *jump activity*, the adjectival form is hardly nec-essary; it is obvious that the simpler term *jumping* is better. When, however, an adjective is necessary yet none comes immediately to mind, a noun may do. For *generate condition*, *generation condition* would therefore suffice; if in this instance one does not like the consecutive words ending in *-ion*, one might simply consider the use of *generation* alone. But when adjectives and nouns do not immediately offer themselves, longer phrases may be required in the interests of clarity. *Remember and forget cues* are obviously *cues for remembering and forgetting*. There is nothing wrong with using preposi-tions to say this. And there is nothing wrong with repeating such longer phrases, as long as they say exactly what one means to say and are grammatically correct. Likewise, whatever the choice, the terminology should be consistent; do not write in the same paragraph—or even in the same paper—of *image instructions, imaging instructions,* and *imagery instructions* when all three mean exactly the same thing. Choose the best term, in this case probably *imaging* instructions, and stick to it.

importantly. *Importantly* should not be a problematic word. In common usage, it usually serves either of two functions. On the one hand, *importantly* can refer to the action of someone who does something with an important air; it is then meant ironically, so that one who does something "importantly" is therefore rarely important at all. On the other hand, *importantly* occurs in the expressions *more importantly* or *most importantly,* which are used to state the more important or most important of two or more arguments. This second usage occurs in scientists' writing as well: *More importantly, however, we believe such poor performance reflects fundamental constraints that many two-dimensional tasks such as this one impose on the haptic system.*[53] Otherwise, one tends to avoid this adverbial form in favor of the corresponding noun or the adjective: *it is important that this finding not be overlooked; the importance of this finding cannot be underestimated.*

Some writers, however, erroneously attempt to use the word *importantly* to add emphasis, often in place of words such as *heavily, strongly, especially, primarily, particularly, principally,* and others. Thus, a writer may state that *the effectiveness of repeated presentations depends importantly on their spacing,* or that *recall depends importantly on contextual cues.* It should go without saying that *importantly* does not really apply in these sentences, because the concept of importance is not relevant to the semantic relationships that they express. A similarly inappropriate application of *importantly* sometimes occurs as a sentence adverb in the initial position: *Importantly, these results provide evidence that facilitation occurs*

when the targets are processed in the context of priming. Note that
the same problem arises here that can arise with the proverbial scapegoat of usage guides, the adverb *hopefully;* because
importantly can mean "in an important way," this sentence
can be construed to mean that the results are providing
evidence in an important manner. But this is not at all what
is meant. The writer presumably intends one of the following
two possibilities: *It is an important fact that these results provide
evidence that facilitation occurs when the targets are processed in
the context of priming,* or, simply, *these results provide important
evidence that facilitation occurs when the targets are processed in
the context of priming.* One would hope that the writer had in
mind the latter alternative: In the first instance, the writer
would be calling too much attention to the importance of his
or her own work, in an awkwardly verbose manner, whereas
in the second instance, the evidence alone is important. Probably the best advice that may be given with respect to the use
of *important* and *importantly* is that these words should occur
sparingly; usually, if something that we have done or have
discovered is truly important, its importance will speak for
itself. (See also INTERESTING TO NOTE.)

increase, increase with. In writing about experimental
psychology, sentences with the verb *increase*—and *decrease*—
are quite common. The analysis of experimental results involves the evaluation of effects and interactions, and
whenever two factors interact, as the magnitude of one of
them either increases or decreases, that of the other will likely
increase or decrease too. On the simplest level, this is merely
another way of describing the relationship between the values of x and the values of y on a graph.

There are many idiomatic ways to express such relationships in English: we say that wisdom increases, or that fine
wines improve, *with age;* that performance improves *through
practice;* that things will get better *over time;* and so on. Note
that these italicized phrases are all prepositional; that a different preposition is used in each case, reflecting the essen-

tially idiomatic nature of prepositions *(with, through, over)*; and that the nouns introduced by the prepositions *(age, practice, time)* in all instances clearly imply a continuing temporal process. That process, semantically embedded within each phrase, could be spelled out in clauses: wisdom increases as one's age increases, fine wines improve as their age increases, performance improves as one adds to the time spent practicing, and things will get better as the years go by. But there is no need to rewrite these prepositional phrases thus, because they are adequately clear on their own, and they are obviously more concise.

Problems arise when the prepositional phrases following a word such as *increase* or *decrease* do not immediately imply such temporal relationships, or when they introduce other semantic ambiguities. If I write that *reaction times decrease with word frequency*, it is not immediately clear whether word frequency is increasing or decreasing; indeed I might only mean that reaction times decrease when word frequency is somehow taken into account. Again, if I write that *reaction times for naming will increase with experimental uncertainty*, I might not mean that uncertainty is increasing at all, but simply that when uncertainty occurs, reaction times will increase. Finally, the prepositional phrase can cause ambiguity in relation to the subject: If I write, for example, that *the perceived speed increases with increases in contrast*, rather than *the perceived speed increases as contrast increases*, I am literally implying that *the speed itself is increasing in contrast*, and this is surely not correct. Some readers will undoubtedly maintain that the contexts will provide the correct meanings in these instances, and that to think otherwise is to engage in semantic hair-splitting. But it is not. In these examples, the prepositional phrases have become vague; why not make them as precise as possible? It is not at all verbose to write, *Reaction times for naming will increase as experimental uncertainty increases;* it is precise and clear. Another solution is slightly more awkward: *Reaction times for naming will increase with increases in experimental uncertainty.* But in the interest of stylistic vigor, the clause *(as experimental uncertainty increases)* is better here than the prepositional phrase *(with increases in experimental uncertainty)*, which in this case is long and un-wieldy.

independent. See ADVERBS VERSUS ADJECTIVES.

-ing words. Words ending in *-ing* are either verbs or verb forms used as other parts of speech. They fall into three categories: (a) the present continuous tense, (b) participles (verbs used as adjectives), and (c) gerunds (verbs used as nouns). Such words, although commonplace, must be handled with care, simply because they can act as more than one part of speech. If the context of an *-ing* word is at all ambiguous, the reader may mistake the word's grammatical function and have to read the sentence at least twice in order to construe it correctly. Obviously, this wastes time.

Consider the following statements regarding the "components" in a model of how one counts a set of objects:

> One <u>component is being able</u> to recite the sequence.... A second <u>component is ordering</u> the objects linearly, such that each object is counted exactly once.... A third <u>component is that the objects have to be isolated and identified</u> as individual units. [54]

In the first two sentences, the subject, *component*, is followed by a verb that the reader at once assumes to be in the present continuous tense *(is being able, is ordering)*. As the reader proceeds past the verb, however, it suddenly becomes clear that *being* and *ordering* are not to be read as expressing tense at all; they are instead gerunds, and so the reader has to reread the sentence in order to construe these words properly. It is not the components that are able to do anything or that are ordering anything; rather, the components actually *are* these two capacities or requirements. Note, too, that the third sentence in the series is perfectly clear; after the verb *is* comes the clause *that the objects have to be isolated and identified as individual units*, which can only be construed as a noun construction (unlike the initially misread gerunds in the first two sentences).

There are several ways to revise the three aforementioned sentences. One would be to adopt in each sentence a construction similar to that in the third one:

> One _component is that one must be able_ to recite the sequence…. A second _component is that one must order_ the objects linearly, such that each object is counted exactly once…. A third component is that the objects have to be isolated and identified as individual units.

Note that in each case, there is a noun clause beginning with _that,_ instead of the _-ing_ word or gerund. This yields three parallel constructions, which reinforces the meaning, but they sound wordy and redundant.

Another alternative would be simply to use nouns if possible, or to choose different verbs so that the gerunds cannot be misconstrued as representing the present continuous tense. The following solution includes both strategies, in the first two sentences, respectively:

> One _component is the ability_ to recite the sequence…. A second _component consists of ordering_ the objects linearly, such that each object is counted exactly once…. A third component is that the objects have to be isolated and identified as individual units.

Lest the reader remain unconvinced about the danger of _-ing_ words on the basis of this single example, here is another:

> In this framework, the _problem_ for a decision maker _is_ not only _selecting_ appropriate decision rules…, but also _one of discriminating_ among mental representations.[55]

In this example, the author means for us to take _problem_ to be the subject, _is_ to be the verb, and _selecting_ to be the gerund. But the reader will inevitably read _is selecting_ as a present continuous tense, so that the problem itself seems to be selecting something, which is of course nonsense. Note that later on the writer has avoided repeating his mistake, by adding the words *one of* before *discriminating*. As a result, *discriminating* can be taken in only one unambiguous way— as a gerund. Corrected, the sentence might read:

> *In this framework, the <u>problem</u> for a decision maker <u>is</u> one not only <u>of selecting</u> appropriate decision rules…, but also <u>of discriminating</u> among mental representations.*

Or one could chose a different verb, delete the pronoun *one*, and pare the subject down as well:

> *In this framework, the decision maker's <u>problem</u> <u>consists</u> not only <u>of selecting</u> appropriate decision rules…, but also <u>of discriminating</u> among mental representations.*

Both of the original examples just given involve errors of PREDICATION; see that entry.

Ambiguity can cause confusion between the gerund and the participle as well. This often occurs whenever the gerund is used to describe an experimental manipulation:

> *The effects of changing strobe frequency for different rotation rates of the wheel are illustrated in Figure 2.*[56]

Does *changing* here act as a gerund, referring to the experimenter's actual alterations of the frequency in order to determine the resulting effects? Or does *changing* act as a participle, referring to the fact that the strobe frequency simply is in the process of changing? Although one may object that in either case the experimenter is responsible for the change that is taking place, this might conceivably not be the case; the sentence is not clear in this regard, and it forces the reader to ponder just a bit too long over how the *-ing* word ought to be construed. A clearer version might read:

> *The effects of changes in strobe frequency on different rotation rates of the wheel are illustrated in Figure 2.*

Here the ambiguity of the original has been erased: changes are changes, and that is that.

Most dangling modifiers consist of initial participial phrases that do not fit with the subject and verb that follow (see the examples given under MODIFICATION). But such phrases do not have to begin a sentence:

> *The monocular task, setting the position so that the peak matched with the dot, could not be quantified.*

Here the writer means that the task is *to set* the position, or that it *consists of setting* the position, or that it is the task *of setting* the position. By setting off the *-ing* phrase with commas, the author almost succeeds, but there is still the nuance that the task, not the understood experimental subject, might be setting the position; again the sensitive reader will hesitate at this point and have to read the sentence over once or twice to be sure of its meaning. Here are four possible revisions:

> *The monocular task of setting the position so that the peak matched with the dot could not be quantified.*

> *The monocular task—to set the position so that the peak matched with the dot—could not be quantified.*

> *The monocular task—that of setting the position so that the peak matched with the dot—could not be quantified.*

> *The monocular task, which consisted of setting the position so that the peak matched with the dot, could not be quantified.*

These alternatives are all grammatically acceptable. The first is the shortest, but the long subject *(the monocular task of setting the position so that the peak matched with the dot)* makes the sentence hard to read. In the next three sentences, the element that follows the subject has been set off, either as an appositive *(to set the position so that the peak matched with the dot; that of setting the position so that the peak matched with the dot)* or as a modifier *(which consisted of setting the position so that the peak matched with the dot).* Of these three, the first is best because it is relatively concise.

Because *-ing* words are so often ambiguous, the best piece of advice regarding their use is that one should use them sparingly. The same advice is often given to young, immature poets, who often like the present continuous tense because of its sound, thereby forgetting that it is more wordy than the ordinary present, and that its impact is less concrete and forceful. One should be wary of participles, and make sure that they do modify what they are supposed to modify. Finally, any time that one begins a sentence with a gerund, one should probably substitute another form of the word if possible. The initial *-ing* can be either a participle or a gerund, so the reader never knows what is to come next. Never begin a sentence thus:

> *Presenting both stimuli on a trial was expected to cause an intermediate effect on the amplitude of the response.*

The reader will at once think that the first word is a participle, and expect the following:

> *Presenting both stimuli on a trial, ...*

In this case, the substitution of another noun will obviate the ambiguity:

> *The presentation of both stimuli on a trial was expected to cause an intermediate effect on the amplitude of the response.*

To limit the use of the gerund in the initial position is probably one of the most important pacts that the scientific writer can resolve to make.

in order to. See PURPOSE, CONSTRUCTION OF.

interactions. See EFFECTS AND INTERACTIONS.

interesting to note. A professor once wrote in the margins of a student's paper that if something was indeed interesting to note, one should let the topic under discussion speak for itself, rather than remind the reader about its being interesting. If the topic is indeed interesting, the reader will figure that out soon enough. Here is a list of openers that illustrate the professor's point:

It is interesting to note that…
It is interesting that…

It is important to note that…
It is important that…

It is worth noting that…
It is noteworthy that…
Note that…

The last of these openers is undoubtedly the best. It contains two words rather than as many as six; it conveys an imperative, yet tempered, sense of urgency; it is not flabby or subjective; it does not leave the writer open to the potential objection that whatever is being noted is scarcely interesting or worth noting at all.

involve. Many scientific writers believe that one should not use the verb *involve,* because it is "a meaningless word." This sentiment is the result of a desire for precision of expression. Yet, surely it makes more sense to say that an *experiment involves a particular procedure* than to say that an *experiment uses a procedure,* or to say that *a procedure involves certain steps* rather than *uses* them. In these instances, *involve* provides a good solution to a peculiar semantic dilemma (see PERSONIFICATION).

J, L

jargon. See NOUNS AND NOMINALIZATION; see also STYLE.

latter, the. One should never write *this latter* or *these latter* instead of the simpler, nonredundant expression *the latter*. *The latter models* are *these models*—that is, the models that have just been referred to; or again, *the latter models* are the latter of two or more previously mentioned sets or types of models. *These* is a "close demonstrative"—that is, it can refer to something that has just been mentioned. To append *latter* to *these* is redundant and hence superfluous.

left-handed. See HYPHENATED TERMS.

lists in text. See COLONS; SEMICOLONS.

long-term. See HYPHENATED TERMS.

lowercase, uppercase. These words are most often used to refer to stimuli consisting of letters on a video screen. Each of these terms should be written as one word, not two, and the hyphen should therefore occur only in constructions like the following: *The stimuli were either lower- or uppercase letters.* For further information, see any good dictionary.

-ly. See HYPHENATED TERMS.

M

maintain. *Maintain* is never an intransitive verb; it always takes an object. Therefore, one can never say that *the increase in hippocampal activity maintained across all experimental sessions.* Instead, one should say that *the increase held,* that it *persisted,* or that it *remained at a certain level*—or perhaps that it *was maintained;* but only if someone or something actually did maintain it. There can be no good reason to endow *maintain* with an intransitive meaning when there are already several commonly accepted, clear and concise words in English that serve the same purpose.

manuscripts, preparation of. For a thorough discussion of preparing manuscripts for submission, all writers should consult the APA manual. The following basic guidelines, however, should always be kept in mind:

1. If a journal recommends a specific style manual, the writer should consult that manual and attempt to follow its recommendations as closely as possible. This is particularly important with regard to policies about abbreviations, citations, and references.

2. An author who is nonetheless unsure of the style expected by the editors of a particular journal should at least skim through some copies of that journal in order to determine what is indeed expected or preferred. In this way, for example, one can quickly determine whether references and citations should be given in chronological or alphabetical order, whether referenced titles are to be abbreviated or spelled out, whether or not factors or interacting variables should be capitalized, whether or not "s" or "sec" is to be used as the abbreviation for *seconds,* and so on. Close scrutiny of the journals published by the Psychonomic Society, for example, will reveal a few such points of difference with the style favored by the APA. In most instances, these are not the result of this particular society's willful independence, but of linguistic change; house styles constantly evolve as the language changes, and as they do so, their conventions can diverge.

3. Manuscripts should be double spaced. This applies to the entire manuscript, including authors' names and affiliations, table and figure captions, authors' notes or acknowledgments, footnotes or endnotes, references, and appendices. This is not an arbitrary requirement. When a copy editor prepares a manuscript for publication, numerous directions must be added for the typesetter, even when the manuscript is flawless and elegant. Authors are seldom aware of the

extensive labor that this entails. For example, every instance of a numeral followed by a measurement (i.e., 3 ms), must be marked so that the two will stand on the same line in the final copy; the same is true of numerals used as parts of names (Day 2, Group 4, etc.). Fonts and font changes are indicated, italics and boldface marked, hyphens added or deleted, dashes of varying lengths specified. On a single-spaced manuscript or a single-spaced portion thereof, no room is left for the copy editor to add such marks, let alone to make whatever emendations may be deemed necessary to put a manuscript into good grammatical shape. Ideally, therefore, all manuscripts should have no more than three lines to the inch.

4. All paragraphs should be indented. It does not help to add an extra space between paragraphs instead of using normal paragraph indentations. If a nonindented paragraph begins a page of a manuscript, it will often be typeset as a continuation of the paragraph that precedes it, and in the final proofs, this is often hard to catch.

5. Personal computers and word processing programs have by now made it possible for the writer to prepare a reasonable facsimile of a typeset copy. Often, however, this is more of a hindrance than a help to copy editors and typesetters. It is their job, not the author's, to design the published text.

a. Use a font that is easy to read. "Times" is a good choice; so are the more modern sans serif fonts.

b. Use one font size throughout. There is no need to type the title or the headings in large print, because this will be determined by the copy editor and typesetter in accordance with a journal's standard format.

c. Always use underlining to signify italics. Often authors want too many words italicized for emphasis, forgetting that the frequent use of italics will very likely distract the reader. It is much easier for a copy editor to indicate the deletion of italics when they are signified by underlining than when they are already set as italics.

It is also much easier for typesetters, who type very fast, to recognize text that is underlined in the manuscript than it is to recognize text that has been italicized with a word processor.

d. Never indicate boldface on the manuscript unless it signifies mathematical entities such as vectors. Copy editors know when headings and subheadings are to be set in boldface and when they are not; authors are seldom well informed about this. Also, journal policies vary; where one journal will require boldface, another will require italics or even plain roman type.

e. All submitted copies of a manuscript should be of good quality, printed on good paper. Too often an author will send in one clear laser-printed copy along with one or two poor xeroxed versions. When the time comes for editing, proofreading, and typesetting, one of the poorer copies often winds up being used for production. This is hard on the eyes of all concerned, which means that the risk of mistakes in production will be increased greatly. Laser copy is always preferable to dot matrix; dot matrix copy should be printed with a new ribbon. Xeroxed versions should be printed clearly, with as vivid contrast as possible.

6. Make sure that approximate locations for all tables and figures are interspersed within the text, and that in the text itself, every figure and table is mentioned at least once.

7. Try to keep abstracts and authors' acknowledgments brief and to the point. Abstracts should be no longer than three quarters of a page, double spaced.

8. Make sure that the text citations and the references correspond; there should be no uncited works on the reference list, and all works cited in the text should be on the reference list too. Check to see that each corresponding citation and reference share the same date.

The preceding guidelines facilitate editorial production almost as much as do perfect grammar, clear style, coherent argument, and lucid thought.

meaning. Sometimes a sentence may be grammatically flawless, yet the meaning will not be what the writer intends at all:

An entry was recorded when all four feet were in an arm.

—Obviously the writer is referring to a four-footed animal and a maze arm here, but because he has forgotten to mention this, the sentence suggests something rather peculiar.

These tasks were designed for the study of defensive burying of mice.

—Are the mice doing the burying, or are they being buried? Of course the mice are engaging in this behavior, but the sentence is too ambiguous for the reader to know.

Weaning of adult mice took place on Day 32.

—Can adult mice be weaned? Certainly not. Without the context, it is not exactly clear what this author might have meant. A good guess would be that the mice were adults when the experiment was performed; prior to that, they were weaned on the 32nd day after birth.

Rats were inescapably shocked.

—Who forced the researcher to shock the rats? The writer actually means that the rats were exposed to, given, or subjected to inescapable shock. But the writer has implied that as a researcher, he or she had no choice.

The relevant data are in Figure 1.

—This statement is false. The data are not in Figure 1 at all; they are somewhere in the researcher's computer or written files. They are, however, *represented* in Figure 1, by means of whatever graphic devices (e.g., the lines or bars in a graph) that figure contains. (Note, too, that if the author were to use a table instead of a figure, it would be preferable to write that the data were *presented*, *given*, or *provided* in the table, or that they could *be found* there, rather than to say that they *were* there, which would imply that they could be found nowhere else.)

The author taught perception with an Apple II microcomputer.

—Is the author teaching perception, or a course in perception? To *teach perception,* other than in the most colloquial sense, literally means to teach one how to perceive, but this is surely not what the author means.

Three seconds separated the onset of each word.

—Separated the onset of each word from what? Was the onset divided into two parts? Or were there 3 seconds from the onset of each word to the onset of the next?

The subjects were seen individually.

—This may be true, but it makes the subjects sound as if they were a doctor's patients, which they were not. In fact, these subjects took a written test. It would therefore be more accurate to write that *the subjects were tested individually.*

To test their memory, subjects were presented with lists of 12 pictures.

—This is a peculiar locution, sanctioned by some researchers. It means that the subjects—here monkeys—were presented with sequences of pictures. But because people are often presented with lists of words, the sequences of pictures are called *lists,* in order to establish an analogy between list memory in animals and list memory in human subjects. Whether such an analogy is valid or not can only be determined by the expert in this field of research. But surely pictures do not occur in lists, unless they have names and the names have been written out in some form.

We developed a monitoring system that eliminated the human observer.

—This is close, but not exactly correct, for the human observer was not really eliminated but simply made unnecessary. Read: *We developed a monitoring system that eliminated the need for a human observer.*

Piglet olfaction seems to play the most critical role in successful

nipple attachment.[57]
—Whose nipples, attached to what?

With the mixed-sex faces, the effect was reversed.
—In this instance, the writer is talking about pairs of faces, one male and one female. But the writer has implied that each face is androgynous.

The length of each sentence ranged from 15 to 20 words.
—No, it did not. Each sentence had only one length. Read: *The lengths of the sentences ranged from 15 to 20 words,* or *The sentences ranged from 15 to 20 words in length.*

These examples should suffice to suggest that during the final stages of proofreading, one should set aside one's paper, let it sit for 3 days, and then read it over to see what one can find. Many sentences should then stand out starkly among the rest, begging for emendation.

measurement, units of. See ABBREVIATIONS OF MEASURE-MENT.

memory for. *Memory for* is jargon for the general activity of memory or types of memory. In common English idiom, a person has *a good memory for facts,* meaning that he or she is able to remember them well; otherwise, a person has a memory, or memories, *of* persons, places, things, or events whether general or specific. Nevertheless, *memory of* is seldom used by experimental psychologists at all, who tend to use *memory for* in all instances. This is unfortunate. It would be more precise to use *memory of* whenever appropriate, and to reserve *memory for* for discussions of mnemonic ability and not for *particular* memories. In this way, useful distinctions in the language can be preserved rather than blended together.

method, methodology. The noun *method* refers to the way in which a person systematically does something; *meth-*

odology, on the other hand, is the *logos*—the reason, theory, or science—of methods. In contemporary usage, this distinction is often overlooked. Thus, the experimenter will refer to *the methodology developed in Experiment 1, the methodologies for studying mental imagery, a replication of Crowder and Morton's experimental methodology, a methodology for the presentation of stimuli*, or *a low-cost methodology for on-line training*. In every one of these instances, the use of *methodology* is incorrect, and *method* or *methods* is called for instead. Why so many writers seem to prefer *methodology* instead of *method* when they are describing specific human strategies is hard to say, but presumably they feel that the longer word is somehow more formal, professional, or serious. To the reader who knows etymologies, on the other hand, *methodology* sounds bombastic when it merely means "method"; it is a hypercorrect form created through the needless addition of syllables, rather like the use of *orientated* instead of *oriented*. The distinction between *method* and *methodology* is useful; if *methodology* is only to mean "method," that distinction will simply drop out of the language. It would be better to try to preserve it.

mixed constructions. Mixed constructions occur less frequently than other grammatical errors, but they can be among the most confusing. The mixed construction consists of two unrelated grammatical constructions conjoined so that together they make no sense. There is no pattern to mixed constructions; with the exception of one simple type, they are unique.

The aforementioned exception is sometimes classified as an error of modification that resembles a dangling modifier in the initial position, and sometimes treated as an error of reference; but in fact it is neither:

> *In Treisman and Gelade's feature-integration theory, they argue that features are combined in a map of locations.*

On the surface, this sentence may at first seem acceptable to some, but it is unclear. The opening phrase—*in Treisman and Gelade's feature-integration theory*—prepares the reader to expect that what follows will be a statement about the contents of the theory, but instead the pronoun *they* refers to Treisman and Gelade, as if they are present in their theory like characters in a story. One revision of this sentence might read as follows:

> *In Treisman and Gelade's feature-integration theory, maps of locations are said to permit the combination of features.*

Here the maps, unlike Treisman and Gelade, are logically part of the theory. The original sentence may therefore be classified as a mixed construction, because its opening phrase can only introduce an independent clause other than that which follows; between the phrase and the clause, the writer has traded that independent clause for another.

To correct the original sentence with as little revision as possible, however, one need only write the following:

> *In their feature-integration theory, Treisman and Gelade argue that features are combined in a map of locations.*

The opening phrase is now a modifier that explains where Treisman and Gelade make their argument; the pronoun *their* looks forward to its "antecedent," which follows. Whenever one begins a sentence about a person's work in this manner, the pronoun should be written in the modifying phrase; the antecedent of the pronoun should be the subject of the ensuing independent clause.

Unfortunately, most mixed constructions are less straightforward than the type just illustrated:

> *Measurements were made at the various levels of stimulus intensity were used.*

This sentence consists of a clause that is correct by itself (*Measurements were made at the various levels of stimulus inten-*

sity), followed by a verb at the end that does not fit *(were used).* In another sentence, this verb might go well with the subject *(Measurements...were used),* but in the present instance, the subject governs another verb already. Ordinarily when a subject governs two verbs, the verbs must be linked in some way—for example, *Measurements were recorded and later analyzed.* But this would not do here. Without knowing the author's wishes, one has only two possibilities: *Measurements made at the various levels of stimulus intensity were used,* or, more economically, *Measurements were made at the various levels of stimulus intensity.*

In the preceding example, the mixed construction consists of the conflation of two verbs without the necessary grammatical linkage. Another type of mixed construction involves the fusion of a subordinate clause with a fragment from what ought to be an independent clause:

> *When there is more than one target can perform above chance by following a simple strategy.*

Note that it is not clear what is meant here; the writer begins with a correctly written adverbial clause but then shifts immediately to a finite verb, so that the adverbial clause seems to occupy the position of the noun or noun phrase that ought to be the subject of the sentence. It is likely that this mixed construction has been caused by the simple typographical omission of the subject of the independent clause, and that the sentence should read as follows:

> *When there is more than one target, subjects can perform above chance by following a simple strategy.*

Yet without consulting the writer, one cannot always be sure.

Most mixed constructions are created by the student or the novice writer who attempts to write a more sophisticated prose than his or her syntactic knowledge of the language permits, and in such cases it is always hard to second-guess the writer. Today, however, mixed constructions are also caused by "word processing": When a writer cuts and pastes portions of text on a computer screen, he or she can easily forget to revise other portions of the text that no longer fit after the cutting and pasting have taken place. This is most likely the origin of the last example just given. Therefore, even skilled writers need to watch out for mixed constructions.

mode, modality. These terms are used, often interchangeably, to refer to modes of mental processing; cognitive psychologists, for example, refer often to the *auditory* and *visual modalities.* A confusion sometimes arises between *mode* and *modality,* however, that seems to be a part of the age-old philosophical debate about the relation between subject and object. That is, if a subject perceives something visually, that which is perceived also appears to have its own independent visual status in some way. To put it more in the experimental psychologist's terms, although still from the lay writer's point of view: A stimulus may be presented in a *visual mode,* meaning quite simply that the subject can see it, or that it is a visible object of perception. At the very same time, the subject apprehends that visual object by means of some structure or process in the brain that is dedicated to the perception of visual stimuli. This structure or process is often called the *visual modality.*

From the reader's or editor's point of view, confusion arises with respect to whether the writer who uses such terms is talking of the visual object perceived or the visualizing subject who is perceiving it. Often it is hard to tell, because many writers apply the terms *mode* and *modality* to both. To the German idealists in the beginning of the 19th century, this would have seemed to represent a familiar philosophical dilemma, which they tended to answer by arguing that subject and object are inseparable simply because no object can be perceived without a perceiving subject and no subject can engage in the act of perception without an object to perceive; hence subject and object are mutually and reciprocally interrelated and interdependent. But experimental psychologists, who deal with objective, measurable phenomena rather than metaphysical problems, need to avoid such tangled complexities as much as possible. When the experimental psychologist applies the terms *mode* and *modality*, interchangeably, to both the act of perception and the thing perceived, it becomes hard for the reader to be sure what the writer is talking about—a physical structure in the brain, a mental structure that the brain somehow contains, or a physical, objective stimulus outside of the brain that the brain is somehow involved in perceiving?

Only the psychologist, not the editor, can decide on how to assign these terms. It would seem, however, that if the word *mode* could be restricted to the mode of presentation of a stimulus (visual, auditory) and if the term *modality* could be restricted to the type of correspondent processing that takes place (visual, auditory), then a great deal of semantic confusion could be easily avoided.

Such semantic ambiguity between terms that signify subject and object arises repeatedly in certain fields of psychology. For example, it is certainly correct to write of *stereoscopic* or *monocular vision*. But does it make sense to refer to motion that is monocularly or stereoscopically perceived as being *monocular motion* or *stereoscopic motion?* How can motion itself be stereoscopic?

modification. When most writers think of modifiers, they think either of individual words such as adverbs or adjectives, or of what are commonly labeled *dangling modifiers*, a perennial scourge of bygone English teachers. These are particular types of modifiers, however, and it is best to approach the term from a more general perspective. In the simplest terms, a modifier is any word or group of words that functions adjectivally or adverbially within a sentence. Thus, the word *response* in the expression *response time* is a noun functioning adjectivally as a modifier, just as the hyphenated adjectives in the expressions *long-term* and *short-*

term memory are also both modifiers. Likewise, in the expression *memory for words,* the prepositional phrase *for words* is an adjectival modifier. In these four examples, the modifying words or phrases answer the question "What kind of?"—that is, "What kind of time?" and "What kind of memory?" It is true that from a linguist's perspective, the adjectival phrases *long-term* and *for words* are very different from one another as modifiers, but from the viewpoint of the writer for whom the traditional concepts of English grammar are useful rhetorical principles, they are not.

Modifiers include not just words and phrases, but also clauses. Any adjectival or adverbial clause is thus a modifier. Any noun phrase or noun clause or indeed any other verbal unit that is used either adverbially or adjectivally is a modifier too. Thus, for example, in the infelicitous expression *the to-be-remembered target,* the infinitive *to be remembered* has been hyphenated to act as an adjective that modifies the noun *target.*

Modifiers work correctly when they can logically modify the word or words to which they are applied; they are faulty when they cannot logically modify what their author wishes them to modify. To test the modifiers in the terms above, one should simply ask, "Can a 'memory' be 'long-term,' 'short-term,' or 'for words?'" Or again, "Can a 'target' be 'to-be-remembered?'" In every case, the answer is "yes," and the modifiers are therefore logical and correct. Another way to put this relationship would be to say that when one asks such a question of a modifier, one simply converts its grammatical relation to the word that it modifies into either a PREDICATION or a STATEMENT. Each of the questions above is a query regarding a PREDICATION, and in each case that PREDICATION turns out to be correct. At the risk of redundancy, here are the basic equations of meaning that these predications contain:

memory = long-term
memory = short-term
memory = for words
target = to-be-remembered

Once one understands the essential equations of meaning that modifiers embody, the notion of the dangling modifier becomes much clearer than is usually the case in grammar textbooks. Consider the following example:

With this in mind, our paper presents three separate experiments.

Here the initial phrase, *with this in mind,* is the dangling modifier, because there is nothing in the sentence that it can logically modify. Given the grammar of the sentence, it modifies the subject, which is the word *paper;* and obviously a *paper* cannot have anything in mind. Note that, given the method of asking questions that is recommended above, in this case one should ask of the modifying phrase, "Can a paper have anything in mind?"—and the answer will of course be, "No, it cannot." Here the underlying semantic relationship that links the modifier with the word that it modifies is the STATEMENT expressed in the verb *have.* To use the analogy of the equation of meaning again,

paper ≠ having this in mind.

Such semantic equations underlie the use of all modifiers in their relations to the words that they modify.

Following are 14 examples; they have been rewritten from sentences in manuscripts originally accepted for publication in Psychonomic Society journals, in order to illustrate problems of modification. After each example, the appropriate question is asked, followed by the corresponding equation of meaning and a correct revision. Sentences 1–5 open with the most common type of dangling modifier, the *-ing* phrase that begins a sentence, modifying the subject. Sentence 6 introduces a variation: Here the dangling modifier is an adverbial clause rather than a phrase.

By moving the mouse, the mark could be located at any point on the horizontal line. (1)
Can a mark move a mouse?

— mark ≠ moving the mouse.

Read: *By moving the mouse, subjects could locate the mark at any point on the horizontal line.*

(Note that the mouse in question is the kind that one uses to control a computer.)

By manipulating the joystick, the cursor could be brought in contact with the hot spot on the screen.   (2)

Can a cursor manipulate a joystick?

— cursor ≠ manipulating the joystick.

Read: *By manipulating the joystick, one could bring the cursor into contact with the hot spot on the screen.*

By comparing the curves for subject performance, the perceptual mechanisms may be seen.   (3)

Can a perceptual mechanism compare a performance curve?

— mechanism ≠ comparing the curves.

Read: *Through comparison of the curves for subject performance, the perceptual mechanisms may be seen.*

After pressing the key, the stimulus pairs were presented one at a time for 2 sec each.   (4)

Can pairs of stimuli press keys?

— pairs of stimuli ≠ pressing a key.

Read: *Each time the subject pressed the key, a single stimulus pair was presented for 2 sec.*

After responding, the stimulus was extinguished.   (5)

Did the stimulus actually respond?

— stimulus ≠ responding.

Read: *After the subject had responded, the stimulus was extinguished.*

When asked the question, "Which is farther away?" subjects' reaction times were significantly related to the following measurements...   (6)

Can one ask a reaction time anything?

— reaction times ≠ asked.

Read: *When the subjects were asked the question, "Which is farther away?" their reaction times were significantly related to the following measurements...*

Being a difficult case, none of the physicians accurately diagnosed the cardiology problem. (7)
Are the physicians a difficult case?
— physicians ≠ their case.
Read: *Because it was a difficult case, none of the physicians accurately diagnosed the cardiology problem.*

Attention varies from a uniform distribution to a focused point. (8)
Can attention be a distribution or a point?
— attention ≠ a distribution or a point.
Read: *Attention varies from being uniformly distributed to being focused on a point.*

Subjects were undergraduate students serving for credit in introductory psychology. (9)
Can students serve for credit in a course?
— students ≠ serving for credit in a course.
Read: *Subjects were undergraduate students who received credit in introductory psychology for participating in the experiment.*

This procedure must take into account the training period when evaluating the effects of the drug on auditory acuity. (10)
(Can "procedures take" anything "into account"? This is a STATEMENT error to begin with.)
Can procedures evaluate anything?
— procedure ≠ evaluating.
Read: *When using this procedure to evaluate the effects of the drug on auditory acuity, one must take into account the training period.*

The memory of amnesics is significantly impaired when tested explicitly, yet appears to be normal when tested implicitly. (11)
Does one test the memory or the amnesics?
— memory ≠ tested.

Read: *When amnesics are tested for explicit memory, their memory seems to be significantly impaired, yet it appears to be normal when they are tested for implicit memory.*

A similar comparison was not significant.   (12)
Is the comparison itself nonsignificant, or is the effect revealed by the comparison nonsignificant?
— comparison ≠ significant.
Read (perhaps): *The effect found in a similar comparison was not significant.*

Reaction times choosing the shorter line are shown in the left panel of the figure.   (13)
Did the reaction times actually choose the stimulus (the shorter line)?
— reaction times ≠ choosing.
Read: *Reaction times for subjects choosing the shorter line are shown in the left panel of the figure.*

The perception of rhythm is constant when played faster or slower.   (14)
Is the perception, or the rhythm, played faster or slower?
— perception ≠ played.
Read: *Rhythm is perceived as being constant whether it is played faster or slower.*

Note with respect to these 14 examples that the pervasive use of the *-ing* form of the verb often gets the writer into trouble. This is the case in Sentences 1-5, 7, 9, 10, and 13. In Sentences 6, 11, and 14, a similar problem occurs with the *-ed* form of the verb. The reader should study these examples carefully. The isolated form ending in *-ing* or *-ed* is not a finite form of the verb; it therefore permits the author to avoid mentioning its subject, and another word in the sentence becomes the implied subject of the verb instead. Consider Sentences 4–6, which I have corrected particularly with this problem in mind: In each corrected instance, I have given the participle a finite form and added the true subject. Writers should strive thus to use finite forms of the verb whenever possible.

Peculiar problems of modification can also occur with the use of infinitives:

> Answers to these questions will help to assess the general applicability and utility of the distinction between implicit and explicit forms of memory.[58]

Here, *to assess* is an infinitive that answers the question "How?"—that is, the question of how the answers will help. Unfortunately, however, only experimenters, not answers, can make assessments. Here is one solution:

> Answers to these questions will help us [to] assess the general applicability and utility of the distinction between implicit and explicit forms of memory.

In this revision, the true subject of the action in the infinitive is now expressed in the pronoun *us;* people, not answers, are now assessing distinctions regarding memory. Here is yet another solution, without the infinitive at all:

> Answers to these questions will help us in our assessment of the general applicability and utility of the distinction between implicit and explicit forms of memory.

Such errors of modification are unique to the particular case; they do not follow any definable pattern as dangling modifiers do. The only defense against them is to make sure that all the words in a sentence are doing only what the semantic equations of the language permit them to do, and no more.

N

necessary. The word *necessary*, like the word REQUIRED, sometimes causes problems when the agent of an action is not expressed:

Longer tests are necessary to observe the effects.

Note that whoever is to observe the effects has been left out of the sentence, and that this makes the concept of necessity seem to hover in a vacuum. This is so, partly because the infinitive *to observe* implies purpose *(in order to observe)* and because in the sentence no one is explicitly mentioned who possesses this purpose. This state of affairs is also complicated by the fact that the sentence calls to mind the idiomatic expression *it is necessary to,* which takes the infinitive; with *necessary to* plus the infinitive, one expects the predication *it is.* The sentence therefore violates the reader's expectations in at least two ways.

The writer presumably intends one of the following:

Longer tests are necessary if one wishes to observe the effects;
Longer tests are necessary if one is to observe the effects;
Longer tests are necessary for one to observe the effects;
For the effects to occur, longer tests are necessary.

Note that in general, something can be necessary to a person but not to a thing. Something can be necessary for a thing to take place, however.

For a similar ambiguity, see REQUIRED.

neither...nor... See EITHER...OR...

not...or... Coordinations introduced by *not* take *or* rather than *nor: These results were not attributed to specific properties of the flavors of either saline or saccharin, nor to stimulus generalization effects among the flavors of saline, saccharin, and casein.* Here, *or* is necessary: *These results were not attributed to specific properties of the flavors of either saline or saccharin or to stimulus generalization effects among the flavors of saline, saccharin, and casein. Nor* either completes the correlative construction *neither...nor,* or it introduces clauses. Thus when two clauses are coordinated, the first of which is negated by *not,* and the second of which is negated separately, *nor* can introduce the second clause: *The effects of group and day were not significant, nor was there a significant interaction between them.*

nouns and nominalization. In 1966, Wilson Follett called attention to the spreading "noun-plague" in contemporary American English; but even in England at the turn of the century, H.W. and F.G. Fowler defined this affliction as "noun rubbish." Such terms denote the tendency, known more neutrally as *nominalization,* whereby phrases and sentences seem more and more to be constructed out of nouns strung together, rather than nouns in combination with other parts of speech, including finite verbs. The result is often an unwieldy style that lacks simplicity, directness, vigor, or clarity. Thus, for example, one may write of *face features* instead of *facial features;* of *science knowledge* instead of *scientific knowledge* or *knowledge of science;* of *process differences* instead of *different processes, differences in processing,* or *differences between processes;* or of *software development techniques* instead of *techniques for* or *means of developing software.* Even when other parts of speech are used to link nouns, ungainly noun phrases often result: *rats that were presented with a novel solution* can thus be reduced to *novel-solution-presented rats.* And when verbs are used, the writer will likely choose the more wordy, abstract, and colorless alternative: *The test produced facilitation in recall* is thus preferred to the simpler, more concise sentence, *The test facilitated recall.*

Some might claim that there is nothing wrong with such

examples of nominalization, and perhaps even that they are simpler and stylistically more economical than the revisions that I have suggested. One such objection common among scientific writers is that the conventional structures of non-scientific formal writing, in which prepositions link nouns, many types of clauses are used instead of noun phrases, and concrete rather than abstract verbs are admired, "seem" to contain "too many words." But nominalization is not merely a matter of style alone, and unless one is naming concrete objects or events *(goal cup, footshock)*, the overuse of nouns seldom yields simplicity. What, then, is wrong with the preceding examples?

The first, *face features,* suggests laziness. The adjective *facial* is already available, but the author has apparently not bothered to think of it. The next two examples, *science knowledge* and *process differences,* are ambiguous. If *science knowledge* means *scientific knowledge,* it signifies a particular type of knowledge that the scientist possesses; if it means *knowledge of science,* it signifies knowledge *about* science, such as that of the historian of science. To refer to either of these meanings with the phrase *science knowledge* is to confuse the reader, who may not immediately understand which meaning is intended. Indeed these are only two nuances of the original phrase; it could also, for example, suggest a body of knowledge that has been systematized in some theoretically scientific manner. As for *process differences,* the connotations *different processes* and *differences in* or *between processes* diverge so greatly that regardless of context, the reader will never be sure what is meant. If one is interested in clear and direct communication, one should never force a reader to sift through several diverging semantic alternatives, unless ambiguity is actually part of one's purpose, as in the writing of poetry. The first flaw of nominalization, therefore, is that it muddies the act of communication by making meanings unclear.

The second problem with nominalization is that it usually suggests the admiration of the abstract at the expense of the concrete. If I write of different processes, I am referring to specific processes that are characterized by specific differences. If I write of differences in or between processes, I am referring to specific differences that characterize specific processes. But if I write of process differences, I am really elevating the notion of differences to the level of an abstraction, which the processes only vaguely qualify. Rather than being precise about what processes and what differences I am referring to, I am being as ambiguous about them as possible. Likewise, if I choose the phrase *software development techniques,* I am again employing the nouns to suggest an abstraction; the specific techniques for developing the software seem relatively unimportant. Again, I am obstructing the act of direct communication with my reader.

We come, then, to the fifth and sixth examples. *Novel-solution-presented rats* is awkward, turgid jargon. It also reflects a peculiarly modern mania for classification even where classification may not be necessary. All one has to do is establish that the rats in a particular group received a novel solution, designate that group with a simple label, and then discuss the solution's effects when it is appropriate to do so. The relatively vivid and concrete alternative, *rats that were presented with a novel solution,* requires the writer to think in terms of clauses rather than nouns and noun phrases; the effort to do so is worthwhile, if the writer does not want the reader to fall asleep. *The test produced facilitation in recall* is also jargon. Note that the verb *produced* is abstract and vague; so is the noun *facilitation.* Together, they are pompous. *The test facilitated recall,* on the other hand, which has exactly the same meaning, consists of fewer words and is much less vague, because the abstract noun *facilitation* has been exchanged for the more vivid verb *facilitate.*

There are probably several reasons why writers or speakers adopt nominalization. First, it is easy to master. As the democratic impulses of American education admit more and more people into the ranks of the "educated," many find themselves needing a quick fix of eloquence and respectability, and the art of stringing nouns together without verbs is easier to learn than are the conventions of style and the rules of grammar. One does not have to read the masters of English literature to be able to practice the art of nominalization. Second, the excessive use of abstract nouns confers a false air of prestige and knowledgeability on the speaker simply because it sounds fancy—at least to those who don't know better. Third, such a style reflects the increasing tendency to empirically analyze and abstractly categorize the minutest details of all aspects of life, from personal and familial relationships to baseball games and tennis matches. Fourth, it follows the natural human tendency to like to name things, and in our time there seem to be more new things to be named than ever before. A problem arises, however, when older things that have perfectly good names become re-named simply in order to make them sound more sophisticated or more respectable. Fifth, at least in the world of politics, nominalization permits politicians to escape responsibility for what they are talking about: As Edwin Newman pointed out years ago, protective reaction strikes are much more palatable to the general public than bombing raids. And the style of political discourse, through the modern media, affects the style of every citizen's written and spoken language.

Scientific writing often seems prone to noun plague. In the scientist's defense, however, it must be said that science constantly requires new expressions with which the scientist can describe newly studied phenomena as well as their effects or the interactions among them. Nominalization may often seem to be a simple means of doing the job. All one can suggest is that the scientific writer should be careful to choose words for naming that are as direct and concrete as possible. *Attention*, for example, may consist of a mental process or processes; it may operate serially and spatially; and its capacity may be limited. But it is probably better not to call it *a limited-capacity spatially serial processor*.

O

on. In written work on scientific experiments, the preposition *on* is idiomatically used in ways that would probably not be acceptable in a nonscientific context. Thus to the experimental scientist, the following phrases are correct: *on the third trial, on the lexical decision task.* The nonscientific writer would expect *in* instead of *on* in either case. The writer should also remember that there is nothing wrong with writing of *research on,* or *experiments done on,* particular problems or phenomena. One does *studies of* such matters, however.

on [the] average. Writers of formal English prose traditionally know this idiom as *on the average;* scientific writers, who often like to omit definite articles, sometimes prefer the foreshortened *on average.* The choice between the two is a matter of style. If one is willing to accept that scientific writers should adhere to the educated lay person's idiom whenever possible, *on the average* offers a useful means of avoiding an example of needless jargon. Thus, *this increment produces, on average, a 10-msec change* should be written as *this increment produces, on the average, a 10-msec change.* Even the writer who prefers the shorter form, however, should attempt to be consistent. To write *on average* and *on the average* within the same paper is both haphazard and imprecise.

one-way, two-way. See HYPHENS, HYPHENATION.

optionally. The word *optionally* should be used sparingly and with care. As a conjunctive or a transitional adverb, it sounds stilted. *The data can be stored on a floppy disk; optionally, they can be transferred to hard disk* is merely a pretentious way of saying that *The data can be stored on either a floppy or a hard disk.* Likewise, *Optionally, subjects could take part in Experiment 4* can be boiled down to the simpler *Participation in Experiment 4 was optional*. The use of *optionally* can also be ambiguous. What does it mean, for example, to say that *subjects served optionally in a third condition?* Does it mean that the subjects had the option of serving in a third condition, or that the subjects actually chose this option? Was the third condition an additional option following the completion of the first two, or was it an option to either of them? In general, one can avoid such complications simply by using the noun *option* or the adjective *optional*, both of which are more likely to define what is optional and what is not.

P, Q

parallelism. Items or concepts listed in pairs or in series should be formally and logically parallel. Grammatically, they should have the same structure. If the pair or series consists of verbs, they should be in the same number, mood, and tense. If it consists of other parts of speech, those parts of speech should be the same too. Nouns should be listed in series with other nouns, adverbs with other adverbs, and so forth; clauses, phrases, and individual words should not be mixed, unless they all function as the same part of speech. A noun may be parallel with a noun phrase or a noun clause, for example, but not with an adverbial phrase or clause.

> The Macintosh is <u>inexpensive</u>, <u>widely used</u>, and <u>has excellent</u> graphics <u>capabilities</u>.

In this sentence, *inexpensive* is an adjective, *used* is a past participle with a preceding adverb, and *has...capabilities* is a predicate, although it is really a clause lacking its subject. The third element obviously does not fit. Yet although *used*, as a participial form, is arguably parallel with the adjective *inexpensive*, its combination with the adverb *widely* suggests that an adjective proper would be still better:

> *The Macintosh is inexpensive and popular, and it has excellent graphics capabilities.*

Here the adjectives *inexpensive* and *popular* now form a parallel pair, and the second clause is also parallel with the first.

To many, the following sentence may seem acceptable, but the sensitive writer knows that the verbs are not parallel, because one of them is in the passive voice and the other is in the simple past tense:

> *This was constructed of black-covered Plexiglas and consisted of a fluid receptacle and an infrared light gate.*[59]

Because both *constructed* and *consisted* end in *-ed*, a reader might at first be led to construe them as being parallel; this, however, would mean that the second verb would be read as part of the hypothetical construction *was consisted,* which is grammatically impossible. This sentence should consist of two parallel independent clauses, rather than a single subject with a parallel compound verb:

> *This was constructed of black-covered Plexiglas; it consisted of a fluid receptacle and an infrared light gate.*

A more peculiar problem of parallelism can occur when one seeks to name conditions, factors, or categories of observation, according to instructions given to, or behaviors exhibited by, subjects. Thus, in an article on the sexually dimorphic behavior of rhesus monkeys, we find a list of 19 terms that summarize a larger "behavioral lexicon of 37 behavioral patterns," which were used to define the monkeys' activities.[60] Among the terms and the patterns to which they were applied are the following:

> *Mount—Combined double-footclasp and no-footclasp mounts (see Goy et al., 1974).*

Present—Orient hindquarters toward another and deviate tail (see Wallen et al., 1981).

Rough play—Combined category including rough-and-tumble play and brief contact play, as defined in Goy et al. (1974).

Groom—As in Altmann (1962).

Subsequent categories include *Threat, Withdraw, Fear grimace, Display, Restrain infant, Contact, Proximity (Prox), Near,* and *Total activity,* among others. This is a disconcerting list. Not only the terms, but also their accompanying definitions are not parallel. The terms include verbs of different types as well as nouns and nouns preceded by adjectives; there is even one adverb or adjective *(near).* And normally in English, one does not use words other than nouns or pronouns to name anything. There is no reason why the authors could not have chosen terms such as *Mounting, Presentation, Rough play, Grooming, Threats, Withdrawal, Grimaces of fear, Displays, Restraint of infants, Contact, Proximal approach, Near approach,* and *Total activity;* to do so would have been far less taxing on the reader. Indeed such a disorderly list can only suggest to the reader that the writers' thoughts are themselves disorderly and less worthy of attention than they should be. Not only that, for the writer such terms may well lead to a thicket of grammatical errors elsewhere, for how can it be possible at all to refer to behavior as "restrain infants"?

Parallel constructions are governed by a basic structural principle: If the elements in the pair or series are both grammatically and logically parallel, initial portions of each item after the first item in the pair or series may be elided, as long as the meaning and the parallel form remain clear. The three phrases in the following series are parallel: *the parameters, the instructions, and the stimuli.* Yet to repeat the word *the* in the second and third phrases is superfluous; if it is removed, the remaining nouns will be understood to follow in parallel from the first use of *the,* and nothing will have been lost: *the parameters, instructions, and stimuli.* Neither example is incorrect, but the second is obviously better because it is less wordy. For the series to be incorrect, on the other hand, it might read thus: *the parameters, instructions, and the stimuli.*

In constructions such as BOTH...AND or EITHER...OR, whatever follows the first of the correlatives must be parallel with whatever follows the second. Thus, *both the behavioral and hippocampal responses* should instead be *both the behavioral and the hippocampal responses.* Similarly, one cannot write of *the effect both for good and poor readers,* because the prepositional phrase *for good [readers]* and the noun phrase *poor readers* are not parallel. Either the effect occurred *both for good and for poor readers,* or it occurred *for both good and poor readers.* The latter is less wordy and therefore best.

As for *either...or,* it is unclear to state that *the tones were either monotonically ascending or descending in pitch,* for this construction does not explain whether the tones were monotically descending or not. Here, the extra word should be added, even if it seems verbose: *the tones were either monotonically ascending or monotonically descending in pitch.* In the following longer example, however, from which the preceding clause was actually taken, the second *or* comes as a surprise: *The tones were either monotonically ascending or descending in pitch or the pitches changed nonmonotonically.* Here apparently the second *or* really completes the construction that begins with *either,* and it introduces a clause. Therefore, *either* must stand at the beginning of the sentence so that the reader knows that the two clauses are parallel: *Either the tones were monotonically ascending or descending in pitch, or the pitches changed nonmonotonically.* Note that now it is clear why *monotically* does not have to be repeated; the first instance of *or* simply links the nouns *ascending* and *descending,* so it does not require parallelism with the elements that follow *either* at all.

passive voice. In the passive voice, the object of the active form of the verb becomes its grammatical subject, and the true subject is either moved to a secondary position as the agent of the action or simply deleted: *In Experiment 1, we* *tested subjects on a two-alternative forced-choice task* thus becomes, in the passive, *In Experiment 1, subjects were tested [by us] on a two-alternative forced-choice task.* That is, whereas in the first sentence, *subjects* is the grammatical object of the active form of the verb *tested,* in the second sentence, it is the grammatical subject of the passive form *were tested.* At the same time, *we,* which was the original subject, has become the implicit agent, expressed in the uninscribed prepositional phrase *by us.*

In nonscientific English, the passive voice can be useful, although many writers prefer not to rely on it too much, except for very specific purposes. They reason as follows: The passive is relatively verbose, indirect, impersonal, and abstract, thus preventing the writer from achieving a concrete, vivid style, and its impersonality allows the writer to present things as having happened without any personal agency. As a result, the passive voice frequently characterizes the jargon of the bureaucrat who seeks absolution from responsibility for morally culpable actions. Likewise, college students often resort to the passive as an impersonal defence against the risks of personal commitment in writing their freshman English papers. The passive voice has therefore come to have a bad press; at one time or another, we have all encountered the prototypical English teacher who has told us, "Never use the passive voice."

Scientific writers, however, use the passive voice frequently, and the writing of the experimental psychologist is no exception to this practice. Because experimental psychologists seek empirically verifiable and replicable findings in order to reveal the processes that constitute human behavior, they are not primarily interested in individual, personal cases as clinical psychologists or psychiatric therapists are. Any experimental psychologist who fears the admonitions of college English teachers should remember that the passive voice is in fact useful in written scientific expression, because it removes the experimenter from the arena of the experiment when there is no reason for the experimenter's presence to be stressed. Often the use of the passive is not wrong at all.

The fear that the passive voice is incorrect even in scientific writing has unfortunately led scientific writers to use other stylistic devices that rule out human agency. This is manifested in the unnecessary personification of scientific and statistical procedures, whereby the personal emerges through inadvertently adopted metaphors, something that one would expect the scientific writer to abhor: *Experiments, studies,* and *procedures*—rather than experimenters—are said to *use* subjects, to *investigate* behavioral phenomena, to *train* rats in running a maze, to *find* results and effects, to *have aims, purposes,* and *goals,* and so forth. For further discussion of this linguistic phenomenon, see PERSONIFICATION.

A very different issue regarding the use of the passive arises in the confusion between the passive voice of the verb that expresses an action and the past participle that describes a state of affairs. If I write, *The house is newly painted,* the word *painted* is a participle that describes the current state of the house; it is not meant to express the action of the house's having been painted. If I write, *The house was painted yesterday,* I am most likely referring to the act of its having been painted, not to its state at that time (the latter could be the case only if by some peculiar dispensation the house was not still *painted* now). For some reason, scientific writers often confuse these two forms. It is thus not uncommon to find a sentence such as *This finding is easily explained,* when the writer in fact means *This finding can easily be explained.* The problem with saying that the finding *is easily explained* is that the verb *is explained* expresses the state of the finding's having been explained, but the adverb *easily* applies to the action of explaining it. In the revised sentence, the substitution of *can be* for *is* makes it clear that the action, not the state, is what the writer means to convey. Here is another example: *Calibration of the detector is easily accomplished with the aid of an oscilloscope.* This is incorrect; if the calibration is accomplished, it is over and done with. The state must be changed to the action, thus: *Calibration of the detector can be accomplished easily with the aid of an oscilloscope.* And again: *This finding is well illustrated through comparing the results of Experiments 2 and 3.* Here too, the phrase *well illustrated* implies that the act of illustration has already been completed and that the writer is referring to a static situation. The act of illustrating should be stressed instead: *This finding can be illustrated well through comparison of the results of Experiments 2 and 3.*

In summary, although the passive voice can be wordy, it can serve a useful purpose. The writer who wishes to avoid it, however, need not resort to allegorical personification of the scientist's activities. The following guidelines may be of help to anyone who wishes to use the active voice instead:

1. Do not be afraid of using personal subjects. With multiple authors, use the first person personal pronoun whenever it is appropriate; for *visual texture segregation was investigated,* substitute *we investigated visual texture segregation.* For third person authors, use the active; there is no need to say that *an alternative procedure was devised by Eriksson,* instead of *Eriksson devised an alternative procedure.*

2. Delete superfluous instances of the passive. To refer to one's own argument, one should not say, impersonally, *It is argued that the face superiority effect depends on information in the pictorial data store;* one should simply let the argument speak for itself: *The face superiority effect depends on information in the pictorial data store.* In like manner, do not use *it is proposed that, it is speculated that,* or *it is suggested that.*

3. When experimental subjects perform actions, let them be the grammatical subjects of sentences. Instead of *words were recalled better,* write *subjects recalled words better.* Instead of *these separate input systems are processed in parallel,* write *subjects process these separate input systems in parallel.*

4. Finally, even when the passive voice is to be retained, do not confuse the past participle that suggests a state with the passive participle that denotes an action.

participles, present. See -ING WORDS.

perception by. It is common to find articles about *perception by* subjects, whether they be budgerigars, cebus monkeys, honeybees, or patients with Parkinson's disease. The locution *perception by* derives from the passive form of the verb: *perceived by.* That targets are *perceived by* subjects makes perfect sense; but in ordinary usage, the word *perception* would take the preposition *of,* so one should at least wonder whether this should not be the case in scientific writing too. *The perception of songbirds,* or *songbirds' perception of tones,* is idiomatic English; *the perception by songbirds of tones* is not. Worse still is the phrase *the perceived durations by subjects,* for *durations* cannot be *by* anybody; this could be rendered either as *the durations perceived by subjects* or *the subjects' perceived durations,* if that is what the writer means. (See also FINDINGS BY, FROM, IN, AND OF.)

periods. The period marks the end of any sentence other than a question. (A sentence may loosely be defined as a grammatically complete and independent unit of thought that contains at least one subject and verb and stands alone.)

Periods are also used with some abbreviations, such as *cf., e.g., etc., et al., i.e.;* in such cases, there is no logical pattern to the period's use. *Cf.* stands for one word, and *etc.* stands for two; but both take the period in the same way. The second word in *ad lib* is abbreviated, but it takes no period. All such abbreviations must be learned individually (see ABBREVIATIONS, LATIN; see also CF., E.G., I.E., VIZ., and VERSUS).

Occasionally in scientific writing, the title of an article will be a complete sentence. Nevertheless, the title should not conclude with a period. A colon should be used to mark the shift from a title to a subtitle, but this does not mean that the subtitle should conclude with a period either. The same rule applies to centered or left flush headings, which are not run into the text; even when such a heading consists of a complete sentence, the period should not be used. Headings that are run into the text, however, and thus begin paragraphs, do take the period (note those in the present book).

personification. Scientific writing is often highly impersonal. Scientific writers often do not like to write in the first person plural (*we*) and almost never in the first person singular (*I*), probably because they are looking for generally applicable, empirically founded principles that seem to govern phenomenal experience. To inject the subjective voice of the experimenter into scientific writing can thus seem to lessen the universality and problematize the scientific objectivity of what is being reported.

One result of the scientific writer's intentional impersonality is the use of the PASSIVE VOICE, much maligned by English teachers, but often of value to the scientific writer nevertheless. Yet perhaps out of guilt about using the passive, scientific writers have also turned to another device, whereby the third person point of view is applied to the experiment itself, thereby personifying it and permitting the adoption of a personal construction that leaves the experimenter out entirely. This technique represents a kind of scientific allegorizing, a mythopoesis of scientific experimentation. Like the computer, which we somehow feel compelled to conceive as a kind of thinking brain, the experiment has become endowed with all the attributes of human agency.

Here are some examples; in each instance, the core STATEMENT is underlined:

The present *study conducted a comparison* between adaptation and paired-contrast effects. (1)

These *experiments sought to investigate* pitch interactions. (2)

This *study used* a graphic ratings scale. (3)

The present *study aims to discover* the effect of ERP amplitude modulations on attentional allocation. (4)

Experiment 1 studied the effects of diazepam. (5)

This *study designed* a procedure similar to that of Johnson et al. (1985). (6)

This *task deployed* the auditory as opposed to the visual modality. (7)

Condition 3 utilized tones with a constant frequency. (8)

The ANOVA found significant differences due to stimulus context. (9)

This series of experiments observed decrements in ERP amplitude. (10)

All of these statements are faulty, because studies, experiments, tasks, and analyses cannot perform such actions; only people can. Many revisions are possible; here are some respective examples:

In the present study, we conducted a comparison between adaptation and paired-contrast effects. (1)

In these experiments, we sought to investigate pitch interactions. (2)

In this study, a graphic ratings scale was used. (3)

In the present study, our aim was to discover the effect of ERP amplitude modulations on attentional allocation. (4)

Experiment 1 was designed so that we could study the effects of diazepam. (5)

We designed a procedure similar to that of Johnson et al. (1985). (6)

In this task, stimuli were presented to both the auditory and the visual modalities. (7)

In Condition 3, the tones had a constant frequency. (8)

The ANOVA yielded significant differences due to stimulus context. (9)

This series of experiments resulted in decrements in ERP amplitude. (10)

It is remarkable how often the scientific writer will prefer to produce the unedited versions of these sentences, almost as if in atonement for the standard impersonality of scientific style. An ingenious literary critic might say that this illustrates how language always has its revenge: The very attempt to depersonalize the scientific style has led to the personalization of the scientific process itself, as if it were a kind of deity. Be this as it may, the second set of sentences should always be recommended over the first. (See also PASSIVE VOICE; PREDICATION, STATEMENT; and PURPOSE, CONSTRUCTION OF.)

pre-. The prefix *pre-* has two primary sets of meanings. On the one hand, it can mean "prior to," as in *prenuptial* ("prior to marriage"), or *prevent* ("arrive before" someone else—an archaic meaning). On the other, it can mean "previously." In this case, however, the prefix often contributes redundancy, particularly in the past participial form of the verb. Why call something *prearranged,* for example, instead of simply *arranged?* In either case, it has been arranged beforehand.

Indeed, largely because of advertisers and marketers, the meaning of "previously" for *pre-* has come to seem foolish and dishonest. The euphemism *preowned car* has been used to refer not to a car that has never been owned by anybody (i.e., a car prior to its being owned), but to one that has been owned before (i.e., what one ordinarily calls a "used" car). This usage has generally been applied to more expensive automobiles, as if to imply that when a Mercedes Benz has been used by a previous owner, it is really not "used" at all.

Because *pre-* can suggest different meanings whenever it is used to coin a word, confusion may result. What does it mean to write the following?—*In order to measure the rats' consumption, preweighed bottles were weighed.* Literally, this could almost suggest that bottles that had not yet been weighed were now being weighed; therefore, one is likely to ask, why not simply say that the bottles were weighed? Of course, this is not what the writer means; but even so, the sentence is terribly redundant in sound if not in meaning. The writer means that the bottles were weighed once before, and once after, the consumption of their contents. But if their contents are the important topic, why not the following?— *The bottles were weighed twice, before and after feedings, in order to determine the rats' consumption.*

As the preceding example shows, the use of words beginning with *pre-* often occurs in discussions of experimental procedure, simply because that is where one needs to describe a sequence of events. One might have, for example, various experimental conditions, in which exposure to a food or a drug is varied. Some rats might be exposed to the food or drug before others; or they might be exposed to the food twice, whereas others might be exposed only once. Those that have been exposed before have been exposed previously; hence the writer will refer to them as *preexposed rats.* This is perhaps acceptable, although again the confusion between *pre-* as "prior to" and *pre-* as "previously" comes to mind. Also, if the rats already have been exposed, one may sometimes wonder why they are not simply called *exposed* rats instead of *preexposed* ones. But the writer, in the interests of avoiding wordiness, may well go further. The rats that are "preexposed" belong to a particular experimental condition, so the writer will likely refer to this as the *preexposed condition,* as if the condition itself has been exposed. And since the rats have been "preexposed" to a food or drug, the same writer will be likely to refer to these as the *preexposed food* or the *preexposed drug,* respectively, which literally implies that the food and drug have been exposed to themselves. At this time, we must raise our eyebrows in despair. Whereas we began with the rats consuming the food or the drug, now the condition, the food, and the drug seem to have done so too. This is semantic mayhem. The only solution is to avoid the use of the prefix *pre-* to mean "previously" when one coins past participial expressions.

predication, statement. Everyone knows that sentences and clauses are groups of words that contain subjects and predicates. But few people understand that the semantic relation between subject and predicate is a fundamental test of how well a writer or speaker uses his or her native language. This relation may be loosely termed *predication,* as it is in some composition textbooks, or it may be divided more precisely into two categories: *predication* and *statement*. As they are used here, these terms designate the two basic classes of English subject–predicate combinations.

A *predication* consists of a clause or a sentence created with a form of the verb *to be* or a linking verb (e.g., *to appear, to look, to seem,* etc.). A statement consists of a clause or a sentence in which the verb can be any verb other than a form of *to be* or a linking verb. All transitive verbs form statements, as do all intransitive verbs that are not linking verbs. All predications and statements may be viewed as equations of meaning, with the verb acting as an equals sign. Thus, to say that *The subjects were students in introductory psychology* means that *subjects = students.* This is a correct predication. In like manner, to say that *The task was a lexical decision* means that *task = lexical decision.* But this is an incorrect predication. Although it is true that a decision or a set of decisions may be required by a task, in English idiom a task is not a decision per se, and it is certainly not a lexical decision. It would be correct to write—although it may seem wordy—that *The task was a lexical decision one,* because in this case *the task* is equated with the task that is implied in the pronoun *one.* If this will not suffice, the sentence must be rewritten, depending on its context. Various possibilities offer themselves, depending on what is meant: *Subjects were given a lexical decision task; In this experiment, the subjects performed a lexical decision task; In this task, the subjects made lexical decisions; The task involved [comprised, consisted of] lexical decisions;* and so forth.

Here is another example of predication: *In Experiment 1, picture naming was faster than word translating.* On the surface, this sentence may seem admissible, but what it really means is that *in Experiment 1, subjects were faster at picture naming than they were at word translating.* Rather than choose the semantic shorthand of the first sentence, one should spell out the facts as they are expressed in the second sentence. It is at best questionable to speak of naming pictures as being fast or slow; it is always correct to refer to people as being fast or slow at doing it. An even less permissible, yet not unusual, shorthand is exhibited in the following predication: *Words were faster than pictures for subjects in Experiment 2.* It simply will not do to speak of any kind of stimulus as being fast or slow, unless one is referring to the speed of stimulus presentation; what is meant here is that the subject is fast or slow in responding.

The following is a faulty statement: *The results of Experiment 2 falsified our hypothesis.* Here the semantic equation is incorrect, because *results* cannot *falsify* anything. *Refuted* or *contradicted* might be substituted for *falsified,* depending on the writer's intention; *refuted* would simply be an acceptable dead metaphor, whereas *falsified* is not. Here is another example: *These data can be omitted and have significantly low error scores.* This too is an incorrect statement; obviously, *data* can be *omitted,* but they cannot *have scores.*

A peculiar instance of fallacious statements involves the PERSONIFICATION of experiments (see also PASSIVE VOICE and PURPOSE). Here one finds statements in which studies, experiments, tasks, trials, and even results do things by way of metaphor that only experimenters do in fact. Thus, studies *examine* factors, experiments *find* results, problems solved by subjects *achieve* a certain probability level, and results *evaluate* models. No matter how tempting, the practice thus exemplified should be avoided. The discussion of analyses and comparisons can lead to similar errors—like experiments, which do not find results, analyses and comparisons do not find effects; they reveal or yield them.

prior to. Most scientific writers seem to prefer the expression *prior to* instead of *before,* perhaps because *prior to* seems to mean "immediately before" and might therefore be more precise. This is a questionable assumption. In many such instances, *before* would suffice, and it often permits the use of a clause instead of a noun or a phrase. Thus, for example, the phrase *prior to receiving instructions* can be rendered not only as the phrase *before receiving instructions,* but also as the clause *before they received instructions;* likewise, *prior to the beginning of the experiment* can be stated more concretely with the clause *before the experiment began.* Because *before* is one word rather than two, because its meaning is more concrete, and because it is much more a part of daily speech, it is often a less pretentious alternative. (Cf. FOLLOWING.)

problematic. Something that is *problematic* is somehow not right; it contains problems. By definition, it is not something that causes problems in or for something else. It is therefore incorrect to write, *The results of the present experiments are problematic for previous findings* [*theories, models, hypotheses, views,* etc.]. Read instead: *The present experiments raise problems with respect to previous findings* [*theories,* etc.], or *The present experiments suggest that there are problems in previous findings* [*theories,* etc.]. There is nothing problematic about these alternatives.

pronouns. *Pronoun Reference or Anaphora.* In traditional English grammar, a pronoun is defined as a word that stands for a noun. In contemporary linguistics, the pronoun is more often viewed as belonging to a subclass of nouns, most of whose members are either "anaphoric" to their antecedents (as *he, she, it, they*) or "deictic" in that they express the identity of the speaker or the addressee of an act of utterance (*I, you, we*).[61] Pronouns can be classified as personal, reflexive, or possessive. In English composition, problems in the use of pronouns arise primarily when the personal or the possessive pronoun participates in an unclear anaphoric relationship. This is what standard handbooks term errors of pronoun reference, which include errors of numerical agreement between the possessive pronoun and its antecedent.

The simplest instance of pronominal anaphora consists of the subject of an independent clause that corresponds to the subject of a preceding independent clause. The two clauses do not have to be parts of the same sentence; they may constitute two sentences in succession. In the following example, the subject *they* thus refers to the subject *Weaver and Bray*, which constitutes its antecedent:

> Then Weaver and Bray in 1930 reported the reproduction of speech in the auditory nerve. <u>They</u> proved that the effect was truly biological and not a mere physical artefact.[62]

Were these two clauses combined within one sentence, the result would be what is traditionally called a compound sentence:

> Then Weaver and Bray in 1930 reported the reproduction of speech in the auditory nerve, and they proved that the effect was truly biological and not a mere physical artefact.

Note that standard conventions of English grammar recommend the comma here before the coordinating conjunction and the anaphoric subject. Many writers, however, seem to prefer to leave the anaphor out, thus:

> Then Weaver and Bray in 1930 reported the reproduction of speech in the auditory nerve, and proved that the effect was truly biological and not a mere physical artefact.

Why this type of construction is so common particularly in scientific writing is open to conjecture, but it is safe to suspect that the lack of the pronomial anaphor may be due to fear of ambiguity; writers are afraid that if they use an anaphor, its relation to the antecedent may not be clear.

Indeed some writers probably worry too much about the ambiguity of the anaphoric pronoun. In the following example—

> These factors strongly influenced the error patterns of the adult readers, and they would very likely influence the errors of younger readers too.

—the anaphor *they* is preceded by three plural nouns, yet only one of them can be construed as the antecedent. This is so, not because the pronoun *they* is unambiguous, but because the parallel structure of the two clauses enables the reader to construe *they* and *these factors* as referring to the same thing. Another anaphoric parallel structure can be seen in the following sentence, in which the anaphor *them*, like its antecedent *the sentences*, functions as an object; again, both words have a common referent:

> *The students then listened to the sentences, after having been instructed to remember them for the test.*

The following sentence contains two anaphoric pronouns, *their* and *they*:

> *The effects of bulbectomy in rats on their radial maze performance might be reduced if they received embryonal brain grafts.*

Here neither of the anaphoric relationships is correct. Possessive pronouns not part of a subject noun phrase are usually anaphoric to the subject of the sentence in which they occur, or to an understood antecedent that has been established in a preceding sentence, but here *the effects* clearly do not constitute the antecedent of *their*, and the antecedent is in fact included in a prepositional phrase (*in rats*). Likewise, since *they* is the subject of the subordinate clause, one would expect its antecedent to be the subject of the preceding independent clause, but again, *the effects* clearly do not constitute the antecedent of *they*. The antecedent of both pronouns is the noun *rats*. A revision might read thus:

> *The effects of bulbectomy on the radial maze performance of rats might be reduced if the rats received embryonal brain grafts.*

Pronouns and "Gender." For the past two decades, the question of reference to sex or "gender" (i.e., not grammatical gender) in English has been hotly debated, and today, most handbooks on English composition recommend that one should attempt to avoid "sexist" language. This is not always a simple matter. Up until the last 10 or 15 years, the masculine third person singular pronoun was used by speakers of English for centuries to refer to both men and women; it was rarely if ever construed to signify the dominance of the male sex, because *man* and *mankind* were terms that served to refer to all human beings in general, and because in English, the pronouns *he, him,* and *his* were arbitrarily used to refer to those words. (In certain other Germanic languages, such terms have always been construed as feminine, but this never led anyone to argue that they signified the dominance of women.) Regardless, however, most people seem now convinced that to use *he* to refer to anyone other than a person of the male sex is improper and unacceptable. This has led to locutions such as *he or she, he/she,* or *s/he,* all of which tend to clutter a writer's prose and make it hard to read. Fortunately for the scientific writer, however, this situation is not nearly as problematic as it can be for writers in other fields. Often one can simply refer to *subjects* and *their tasks* and thus avoid the question of gender entirely by sticking to the plural (unless of course the subjects' sex is a factor in the experiment under discussion). From time to time, if *subject* must be used in the singular, one can write of *each subject* or *the subject* and *his or her* performance simply to remind the reader that both men and women participated. If used sparingly, *he or she* and *his or her* can be easily accommodated within a graceful prose style. If used too much, these phrases will simply crowd one's prose with unnecessarily obtrusive words.

Occasionally, a politically minded writer will attempt to use the pronoun *she* alone to refer to a subject who is a generic example, after the manner of polemical scholars in the humanities who use *she* wherever *he* would have been the norm in years past. But unless the particular subject to whom one is referring really was a woman, this is just as misleading as it might be to use the pronoun *he* in the same instance. Scientific writing deals with empirical observations, not political agendas, unless one is writing to justify one's science within a political context. If one wishes to remind the reader that women are included equally with men, one should simply use the pronouns *he* and *she* together, despite the stylistic infelicities alluded to earlier. To use *she* to refer generically to both men and women is stilted and confusing.

In certain specific instances, one can draw on other European languages for help. In many such languages, for example, parts of the body are accompanied by the definite article rather than the possessive pronoun. Thus a simple solution to problems of "sexism" in scientific English might in many instances be to use the definite article in English too: *Each subject was told to fix the eyes on the target; the subject raised the right hand;* and so forth. Although such expressions may yet sound a bit foreign, they can be useful, and it is not hard to envision their becoming a customary part of the language in the future.

punctuation. For most matters of punctuation, one should resort to any grammar handbook. All of them contain similar information about punctuation, and all of them present it in a similar manner (see the Bibliography for some useful examples). For specific points regarding the punctuation of scientific writing, see COLONS, COMMAS, DASHES, EXCLAMATION MARKS, PERIODS, SEMICOLONS, and QUESTION MARKS.

purpose. Experiments, studies, tasks, conditions, and trials do not have purposes. Experimenters do. Thus, it is an incorrect PREDICATION to write that *the purpose of this condition was to determine...* or *the purpose of the present experiments was to examine...* As it is presented in the first instance, the condition has the purpose, and the condition's purpose is to determine something; in the second instance, the experiments have the purpose, which is to examine something. But experiments do not determine or examine anything at all; only experimenters can do these things. Various correct alternatives offer themselves: *we intended to use this condition to determine...; we used this condition to determine...; this condition was used to determine...; our purpose in performing the present* *experiments was to…; our purpose in the present experiments was to…;* and so forth. Here is an elegant way in which three authors chose to deal with the purpose that lay behind their experiment:

> *The present experiment was designed for two purposes. First, given the counterintuitive nature of the expectations and the fact that not all investigators have obtained evidence that visual scans of consonant arrays are self-terminating…it seemed important to replicate the previously obtained…effect.*
>
> *More important, however, was the need to examine the stronger prediction from the model that the reason subjects use a memory search for scanning the contents of visually displayed words is that it is the only type of scan that would be possible and that its use is not strategically determined.*[63]

Note that the purpose introduced in the first sentence is not that of the experiment, but rather that of the implied experimenters; the experiment was designed and ultimately carried out in the service of (i.e., *for*) their purposes, not as if it had a life of its own. When the specific purposes or needs are stated in the next sentences, it is again clear that they were those of the experimenters: *it seemed important* [i.e., to the experimenters] *to replicate the effect,* and there was *a need* [i.e., on the part of the experimenters] *to examine the stronger prediction.* All of these statements are logical, whereas the notion that experiments can possess purposes is not.

One might object that to write *the purpose of Experiment 3 was to test whether there would be an effect of…*is acceptable idiom within the context of scientific writing, and this is certainly an arguable case. But coupled with the tendency to personify experiments in locutions such as *Experiment 3 tested,* or *the present experiments examined,* such word choice seems to suggest a rather odd choice of metaphor. Having attempted to banish personal pronouns by writing in the passive voice, scientists have instead let subjectivity in the back door in the form of personified experiments. Since this tendency to personalize is therefore apparently irresistible, why not simply give in to it and write in the first person instead? *We designed the present experiment for two purposes* is excellent English. (See also PERSONIFICATION; PREDICATION, STATEMENT; and, below, PURPOSE, CONSTRUCTION OF.)

purpose, construction of. In English, the sign of the construction of purpose is the phrase *in order to* followed by the infinitive; often the words *in order* are dropped out, leaving simply *to* with the infinitive. *So that*, on the other hand, expresses result, which is not the same as purpose.

For a purpose to be expressed clearly and correctly, it must follow from the personal subject and verb from which it proceeds:

> *We performed this experiment [in order] to investigate whether or not electrophysiological responses to repeated events might provide an implicit test of memory.*

We is the subject of the verb *performed*, but it is understood that *we* governs the verb *investigate* as well. Another way to put this relationship, although it would sound excessively formal, would be to say that *We performed this experiment in order that we might investigate whether or not electrophysiological responses to repeated events would provide an implicit test of memory*. This version is wordy of course. But it provides the writer with a useful test. Whenever a construction of purpose that consists of *to* or *in order to* plus the infinitive can be translated into *in order that* plus a modal clause, one knows that the original construction is correct.

The word order of the sentence just given can be reversed without ambiguity:

> *[In order] to increase our database, we carried out further tests.*

Note that again the subject is *we*, the experimenters whose purpose it is to increase the database, and that again the suggested test can be applied to determine whether or not the construction is correct: *In order that we might increase our database, we carried out further tests.*

Errors thus occur when the subject or the agent of purpose is simply left out:

> *In order to retrieve the target information, the context at test must be the same as the context at training.*

Here, *context* is the subject of the sentence, so that the purpose introduced by *in order to* suggests that the *context* itself will actually retrieve the target information; the construction of purpose thus contains an implicit incorrect statement. The simplest way to revise this false equation of meaning is to add the personal agent:

> *In order for subjects to retrieve the target information, the context at test must be the same as the context at training.*

Because scientists like to write in the passive voice, the construction of purpose will often follow a verb in the passive, as when experiments are initially introduced. This can lead to trouble:

> *This study was designed to investigate bias invariance.*

Here it sounds as if the study was intended to do the investigation on its own, without any help from the experimenter; even the fact that the experimenter is the implied agent of the passive verb does not help. The sentence means either of the following: *This study was designed for the purpose of investigating bias invariance,* or *We designed this study in order to investigate bias invariance.* Although this difference may seem subtle, it is in fact a difference between what does, and what does not, make sense. Writers should be wary of statements such as *Experiment 1 was designed to…, These experiments were carried out to…,* and others like them.

One must also guard against the use of the construction of purpose in which the agent of the action is switched in midstream:

> *To test these theoretical predictions, the subjects judged whether the targets were "same" or "different" while the symmetry of the background was varied.*

In this sentence, the phrase *to test these theoretical predictions* literally expresses the purpose of the subjects themselves, who are said to be not only making the judgments, but also testing the theory as if to do so were their own idea. But this is not at all what the author means. The purpose is in fact the experimenter's, which the subjects merely carried out by participating in the test. Here are two possible revisions:

> *We tested these theoretical predictions by having the subjects judge whether the targets were "same" or "different" while we varied the symmetry of the background.*

> *To test these theoretical predictions, the subjects were required to judge whether the targets were "same" or "different" while the symmetry of the background was varied.*

questions and question marks. Question marks should be used sparingly. It is usually possible to put questions into the indirect, rather than the direct form, and to save the direct questions for the rare, and hence striking, rhetorical effect. Never mix the two. Do not write, *In this experiment, we asked would delay in postoperative testing affect recovery?* The direct form of this question would be, simply, *Would delay in postoperative testing affect recovery?* The indirect form is the following: *In this experiment, we asked whether delay in postoperative testing would affect recovery.*

R

reaction time. *Reaction time,* like *response time,* is abbreviated as RT. Some researchers prefer the term *reaction time;* some prefer *response time;* some will use either term, depending on their sense of these words' nuances of meaning. Still others, however, appear to use the terms interchangeably. Regardless of the merits of either term, the writer should use them consistently. One should not mingle terms such as *reaction time* and *response time,* about which there are differences of opinion, simply to avoid stylistic repetition. In the beginning of a paper, the writer should choose one of the two and then stick to it. If *reaction time* or *response time* is to be abbreviated, the term should be spelled out on first use, with the abbreviation immediately following in parentheses; from that point on, the abbreviation alone will suffice. If one chooses not to use the abbreviation, one should remember that inconsistency in the use of terms suggests a carelessness on the writer's part.

Reaction times or response times may be *long* or *short, fast* or *slow* (by analogy with fast or slow times in races), *longer* or *shorter,* or *faster* or *slower*—and perhaps even *greater;* but they can never be *larger* or *smaller.*

(See also REPETITION and STIMULUS–RESPONSE LANGUAGE.)

reference. See PRONOUNS.

refers to. The verbal construction *refers to* is often used when a writer introduces a term in order to explain it. In such instances, the term itself should be italicized (it is here underlined for the purpose of illustration):

> <u>Visual direction constancy</u> refers to the ability of the human perceptual system to maintain a stable perception of the direction of an object, relative to the perceiving subject.

Another way to write this sentence would be to remind the reader still more literally that the reason for the italics (here underlined) is in fact that they signify a term to be defined:

> The term <u>visual direction constancy</u> refers to the ability of the

human perceptual system to maintain a stable perception of the direction of an object, relative to the perceiving subject.

Whenever a word is used as a linguistic example, it should be italicized.

repeated measures. This term need not take the hyphen, even when it is used as an adjective: *a three-way repeated measures ANOVA.* (See also HYPHENATED TERMS.)

repetition. At some point in his or her education, nearly every writer has encountered the proverbial English teacher who repeatedly counsels student writers to avoid redundancy and repetition. The term *redundancy* signifies that a writer is repeating ideas needlessly, as if unable to say something concisely and adequately and get on to the next point; the principle that redundancy should be avoided speaks for itself. The term *repetition,* however, refers simply to the repeated use of particular words. To some extent, the advice against repetition is culturally conditioned: The best writers in ancient Greece, for example, thought that the repeated use of good terms was better than a needless quest after synonyms. The writers of modern English essays, however, usually consider repetition to be the sign of an immature style.

Scientific writing, however, is different. The experimental scientist attempts to study phenomena in terms of their effects and interactions; then, in writing, the scientist must explain the problem considered, describe the experimental design and procedures, and provide and interpret the results. Once scientists generally agree on a term to refer to a specific, experimentally established phenomenon, there is no reason to seek other terms to designate it, unless new discoveries have been made, leading to further qualifications or modifications in what was previously thought to be the case. Therefore, by definition, scientific writing is supposed to include some repetition. It is better to use one term repeatedly, or to state it once and then use an abbreviation for it throughout a paper, than to vary the term with imprecision. Synonyms should never be used to avoid the repetition of important terms in scientific writing.

required. In scientific writing, a peculiar ambiguity can attach itself to the word *required*. This is because English idiom allows that people or animals can be required to do things, but that things cannot. We cannot *require* a machine of any kind, including a computer, to do anything, for example. Yet scientific writers, because they often omit personal agents from sentences, often violate this rule.

> *These procedures were required to achieve transfer.*

Here the writer is suggesting that the procedures themselves were intended to achieve the transfer, even though in fact it was the subjects who did so. This is because *required* idiomatically takes *to* when it follows a personal subject *(John was required to take the test over)*. Even if the infinitive *to achieve* suggests a human agent, there is no human agent mentioned in the sentence, and so the reader has no choice but to construe that the procedures have become personified. The writer of the sentence presumably means one of the following:

> *These procedures were required in order for the subjects to achieve transfer.*
>
> *These procedures were required so that the subjects could achieve transfer.*

Here is another example:

> *Further studies will be required to confirm the hypothesis.*

Again, it sounds as if the studies will be ordered to obtain the experimental confirmation, but in fact they will not; they will be carried out by experimenters whose purpose it will be to confirm the hypothesis themselves. Alternatives might include the following:

We will have to do further studies to confirm the hypothesis.

Further studies will have to be performed to confirm the hypothesis.

(See also NECESSARY.)

response time, response times. See REACTION TIME.

right-handed. See HYPHENS, HYPHENATION.

run (verb and noun). There are many ways to use the verb *run*. Just as one can run—that is, operate—a machine, when one carries out or performs an experiment one can *run a series sessions* or *run a test*. Likewise, a person can *run a race*, and a rat can *run a maze*. Slightly peculiar, although certainly acceptable, is the assertion that *the rats were run for three sessions each day*, which really means that the rats were tested in three sessions daily. It seems less appropriate, however, to suggest that *human* subjects are run in experiments; people are not rats, nor are they usually tested in mazes. Still more peculiar is the assertion that *fifteen subjects ran in Experiment 3, as if they were actually running in a competition of some sort. In experiments, human subjects take part*, they *participate*, or they *are tested;* they do not run, and they are not run either.

S

same as, the. See COMPARISON.

same–different. Often in psychological experiments, elements within stimulus arrays vary according to whether they are the same as, or different from, one another; letter pairs, for example, may consist of identical or of different letters. These can be referred to as *same-letter pairs* or *different-letter pairs*, respectively. The terms *same* and *different*, however, sometimes lead to ambiguity. If, for example, one writes *same pairs* for *same-letter pairs* or *pairs with identical letters, same conditions* for *conditions in which there were same-letter pairs*, or *same trials* for *trials in which there were same-letter pairs*, the reader may wonder what the pairs, the conditions, and the trials are indeed the same as. The tendency to employ locutions such as *the same conditions* when one does not at all mean that the conditions themselves were the same results from the natural desire to avoid repetition. There are only two ways to deal with this ambiguity. Either one must spell out what one means in every instance (i.e., write *conditions in which there were same-letter pairs*, or some other such expression), or one must show that *same* is to be read in a semantically egregious manner. Writers often resolve this dilemma by putting *same* and *different* in italics. One should use quotation marks, on the other hand, only to report what someone has actually said—that is, to let the reader know that subjects responded "same" or "different" when they were confronted with the stimuli. Otherwise, subjects make *same* as opposed to *different* responses.[64]

same, the, vs. this same. The expression *this same* is usually redundant. In the sentence *This same pattern held for subjects in all of the learning conditions*, the words *same* and *this* both refer back to a pattern just mentioned. *The same pattern held for subjects in all of the learning conditions* and *This pattern held for subjects in all of the learning conditions* mean the same thing; both are preferable to the sentence that begins with *this same*.

see (vs. cf. or e.g.). In citations within the text, directions within the parenthetical citation are often helpful along with the names of authors and the dates of the works cited; the cited works may be examples, they may be works that the reader is requested to compare with what is presently under discussion, or they may be works that the writer thinks the reader should consider. If the cited works are examples, within the parenthetical citation they should be introduced by *e.g.*: *Although Healey and her colleagues (e.g., Drewnoski, 1978; Healy, Oliver, & McNamara, 1987) have provided impressive evidence…, it appears that…* Note that what follows *e.g.* must truly be an example or examples of what has just been mentioned (in this case, Healey's colleagues). If the reader ought particularly to look at the works cited, within the parenthetical citation they may be introduced by *see*: *With a single-word presentation, a word frequency advantage is occasionally obtained (see Healey, Olivier, & McNamara, 1987).*[65] Or again: *Although positive results certainly have been reported (see Ernest, 1977, for a review), a number of studies have been unsuccessful in showing a relationship between variations in imagery ability and task performance (see J.T.E. Richardson, 1980, pp. 117–142).*[66] If the reader ought to look at the parenthetically cited works not just as relevant studies but as examples, they should be introduced by *see, e.g.*: *The process of attention is often regarded as a direct allocation of some limited processing resource to certain selected information (see, e.g., Broadbent, 1958; Deutsch & Deutsch, 1963; Kahneman, 1973; Keele, 1973; Norman, 1968; Norman & Bobrow, 1975; Shiffrin & Schneider, 1977).*[67] Note that in this citation, *e.g.* by itself would not do, because the preceding sentence does not contain any word (i.e., *researchers, colleagues, investigators,* etc.) that the subsequent names and dates literally exemplify. This logical relationship is often overlooked, with *e.g.* being used indiscriminately regardless of its context. *See,* therefore, does not correspond to any abbreviation; and it does not mean *cf., e.g.,* or *i.e.* (See also ABBREVIATIONS, LATIN; and see CF., I.E., VIZ., and VERSUS.)

semicolons. *Semicolons with Coordinated Clauses.* Semicolons are primarily used to link—that is, to coordinate—independent clauses; in this way, they allow the writer to form compound sentences without using the comma followed by *and, but, for, or, nor, so,* or *yet.* The coordinated clauses can be symmetrical, implicitly expressing either a comparison or a contrast: *On trials when the target was an onset, reaction time should have been fast; on trials when the distractor was an onset, subjects' attention should have been captured by the distractor in the uncued position.*[68] They can be parallel in meaning, but with the second clause adding further information about what has been established in the first: *As an alphabetic orthography, written English systematically encodes information about pronunciation; however, the correspondences between spelling and pronunciation are inconsistent...*[69] Note that in this instance, the transitional word *however* effects the contrast, and that such words or phrases follow the semicolon, never a comma. In general, the clauses coordinated with the semicolon express the same logical relationships that the coordinating conjunctions convey. The following example, with *thus, gives a result: Any event may be assigned any tag; thus the order of presenting events is irrelevant...*[70] And the following example, *with a transitional prepositional phrase, presents specification: The other reason is that it may throw light on general mechanisms that determine how prior experience affects performance; in particular, it is of interest here to understand how the repetition effect is related to our memory for prior episodes.*[71]

Semicolons with Lists. Lists of more than two items that consist of long phrases or clauses are usually divided up with semicolons instead of commas:

> *Following the distribution of these materials, the experimenter read aloud detailed instructions that, in essence, informed the subjects that the experiment consisted of three phases: (1) the study phase, in which they would see the list of the words to be remembered; (2) a 2-min computational phase, in which they would complete some simple three-digit multiplication problems; and (3) a test phase, in which they would open their booklets, find a single word in the middle of each page and the words "old" and "new" in the bottom corners of each page, and circle the word "old" for words they remembered seeing previously in the study phase or circle the*

word "new" for words they did not remember seeing previously.[72]

Note that because of the length of this list, and because in the third item of the list there is yet another three-item list as well, the authors have chosen to include numerals as well as semicolons to divide the material. This is seldom necessary, but in the present instance it certainly helps. (See also COM-MAS, and particularly *Commas and coordination: Compound sentences and compound verbs or predicates.*)

similar to. See COMPARISON.

since. *Since* has both a causal and a temporal sense; both usages are acceptable and useful, even though not that many scientists appear to use *since* to express either of these relationships in their writings. The causal *since* is less emphatic than *because,* which always introduces a cause, whereas *since* can also introduce a reason. In the following sentence, *since* can therefore be substituted for *as: As [Since] preliminary analyses failed to yield reliable differences between male and female subjects, these data were pooled for further analysis.* Here the failure is the reason for, not the cause of, the pooling of the data. Indeed, whenever *as* is used to state the reason for anything, *since* is the better choice. When *since* introduces a temporal clause, the verb in that clause takes the past tense; the verb in the independent clause takes the present or past perfect: *We have gained more students since we dropped that requirement.* (See AS.)

so that, such that. In scientific writing, a common point of confusion is the difference between the expressions *so that* and *such that.* *So that* is an adverbial construction that introduces clauses of result: *The students were given the instructions 1 week before the test, so that they could have plenty of time to plan their strategies.* Here an act has been performed (the distribution of the instructions), from which a result can follow (the possibility of preparing in a certain way). *Such that,* on the other hand, should never be used adverbially; in standard formal English, it is always adjectival. The following example is therefore incorrect: *The amplitude was varied such that its ratio to the period had four possible values.* Here the clause introduced by *such that* erroneously tells us in what way (i.e., how) the amplitude was varied, but *How?* or *In what way?* are questions that can only be asked of adverbs. Either *such that* must be changed to *in such a way that,* which is truly adverbial, or, if result actually is intended, *so that* may be used instead. Thus, just as *so that* expresses the adverbial relation of result, *in such a way that* expresses the adverbial relation of manner. *Such that,* on the other hand, should only answer to the question asked of adjectives, *What kind of?*—*The article's length is such that it should fit within the journal's four-page maximum.*

spelling. In my experience, writers of scientific papers do not often make spelling mistakes, other than the occasional slip. A few minor points of spelling, however, are nevertheless worth keeping in mind; they are intended especially for writers submitting their work for publication, but some of them are applicable to students' writing as well.

1. Both writers of British English who intend to publish work in American journals and American writers who intend to publish in British journals should remember the differences between British and American spellings. In American English, one writes *color, behavior,* and *analyze,* not *colour, behaviour,* or *analyse.* Some journals will accept the British variant of such words in one paper and the American variant in another; others will attempt to regularize such spellings from paper to paper. Regardless of the publisher's capability of computer spell checking, the author who adapts his or her spelling before submitting a manuscript makes the copy editor's job easier.

2. All writers should take care to preserve British spellings in direct quotations in the text or in titles on the reference list. Many journals have the word *behavior* in their titles; it can be spelled with either *-or* or *-our.* If such works are on the

reference list, one should be especially careful in proofreading the final copy. (Note, too, that whether or not a journal is published in England does not necessarily mean that *behavior* will take the *-ou* in the title; consider the titles published by Pergamon Press.)

3. The policy of journals and journal editors can vary widely with respect to certain spellings. Usually the writer will be urged to follow the spellings in a particular dictionary; *Webster's New Collegiate* is a common standard, but when it does not suffice, one may turn to *Webster's Third New International.* (The titles of these dictionaries are important; many readers do not realize that the name *Webster* appears on other dictionaries that are not published by the Merriam company). When the dictionary provides variant spellings, it is always simplest to choose the first, even if the variants are given as "equal." Common points of contention include the dropping of the "e" in *judgment,* the single as opposed to the double consonant in words such as *benefited, focused, modeled, signaled,* or *traveled,* or the dropping of the "e" in *cuing.* Regardless of one's personal preference, the journal's policy should be followed in such instances.

4. Do not use contractions. Write *cannot,* rather than *can't, is not,* rather than *isn't, it is,* rather than *it's,* and so forth. Remember too that *cannot* is one word, not two.

5. Always remember the difference between the homonyms *there* and *their.*

6. Do not confuse common nouns and patented proper names: *Plexiglas* has one "s" and is capitalized; *Teflon* is capitalized; *White Carneau* takes the uppercase "W" (in the plural, it is *White Carneaux*).

7. Do not rely solely on a computer program for checking your spelling. As long as a word is spelled correctly, the computer will register it as being correct, even if it is the wrong word. Thus, if one types *if* instead of *of,* for example, the spell checker will ignore it.

(See also APOSTROPHES.)

stand-alone. This infelicitous adjectival expression can sometimes be ambiguous. What, for example, is a *stand-alone laboratory course in experimental psychology?* A course with no prerequisites? A lab course for nonmajors? A one-semester course that is not part of a two-semester sequence? A course held entirely as a lab, without any accompanying lectures? Presumably it is simply *a laboratory course in experimental psychology.* Or again, what is a *stand-alone personal computer,* other than a personal computer? Do personal computers ever *not* "stand alone," even if they are hooked up or "networked" together? The writer who wishes to use the term *stand-alone* should at least consider other words such as *single, individual, separate,* or *unique* instead. If *stand-alone* is to be used at all, it should be reserved for pieces of equipment, and especially for computer hardware—but not simply for a personal computer.

statement. See PREDICATION, STATEMENT.

stimulus–response language. In scientific behavioral experiments, stimuli are presented to subjects, who then respond to the stimuli in some way. We say that the subject responds, makes a response, or reacts to the stimulus or to its presentation. Note that the verbs *to respond* and *to react,* as well as the nouns *response* and *reaction,* take the preposition *to.* This fact has led to a kind of shorthand, which consists of expressions such as *response times to…* (for *times of responses to…*), *reaction times to…* (for *times of reactions to…*), *RTs to…* (for *times of reactions [responses] to…*), and so forth, all followed by nouns referring to the stimulus in question. By analogy, one finds the expression *latency to…* Yet these expressions are slightly peculiar. Ordinarily the preposition *to* immediately follows the noun that governs it (as in *responses to stimuli*); but when one writes of *response times to stimuli,* that noun has been made into an adjective that modifies another intervening noun. Thus, if one writes of *response* *times to stimuli,* this phrase really means that the *times* are somehow *to the stimuli,* when in fact the writer is describing the *responses* to them. By combining the words *response* and *time* in one expression that concludes with *to,* the writer has confused the semantic function of the preposition, thereby creating an ambiguity that can force the reader to hesitate slightly every time he or she comes upon this term. Of course one can argue that this is acceptable jargon, and that everyone who uses such expressions knows what they mean; but it is also true that such usage is marked by a semantic and grammatical illogicality that one might be able to avoid.

Not only that; by extension, anything that constitutes a response has come to be followed by the preposition *to,* even if the particular word for the response would not ordinarily take that preposition at all. The expression *ERPs to...* (for *event-related brain potentials to...*) is a good example. But one can easily find that pigeons will peck *keys to a light,* that people make *judgments to the recency of the picture of a face,* that rats may experience increases in *fear to cat odors,* that a subject can behave *discriminatively to Stimuli A and B,* that subjects can give *frequency counts to attributes of actions,* and that *people's choice proportions to the 15 full symptom patterns tended to approximate the normative probabilities of the rare disease, given each pattern.*[73] In each of these examples, the preposition *to* has been made to take the place of the phrase *in response to,* sometimes with unfortunate results. In English, one does not make a judgment to anything, for example, nor does one ever experience fear to anything; and one cannot logically give a frequency count to an attribute, unless that attribute is an animate being of some sort to whom one states or hands the frequency count. In all these instances, responses have been made to some sort of a stimulus, but the words for the responses do not normally permit such constructions. This practice, despite its prevalence, is therefore ungrammatical. Judgments are made in response to pictures of faces; event-related brain potentials occur in response to particular stimuli; and pigeons simply peck keys when they see lights (i.e., in response to them). The preceding three statements are not wordy. They are clear, grammatical, and precise.

study, studies. See EXPERIMENT, EXPERIMENTS.

style. In the writing of nonfictional prose, the term *style* refers to the way in which a writer puts words together to make phrases, clauses, sentences, paragraphs, and sequences of paragraphs; style comprises all the words that the writer has chosen to use, and all the ways in which the writer has chosen to organize them. Style includes grammar, but it is more than that. Because every aspect of style reflects the writer's choices, style can be viewed as an implicit, personal signature that pervades the writer's work.

Scientific writing, however, is primarily a means of informing readers about experimental investigations and their results, although occasionally the scientist may write a review of the theories that have been applied to the results in a given field. As a writer, the scientist is therefore most often interested in the communication of apparently objective knowledge or of the objective experience—scientific experimentation—through which that knowledge has been obtained. Scientific experimentation is rigorously controlled and systematized according to well-defined procedures; the scientist's goal is to obtain findings that can be replicated and, in the experimental psychologist's case, to establish what appear to be patterns or principles of human or animal behavior. The scientist who writes about experiments is therefore scarcely interested in expressing his or her personality in prose. If style is the author's signature, the scientist is more likely to aspire to writing with the collective signature of all scientists who are working in a given field, all of whom engage in similar investigations, pursue common goals, and write about their findings as having at least provisional validity. No matter who might write about a given experiment, the style will therefore remain pretty much the same, because the experiment, not the experimenter, is what counts.

Impersonality in scientific writing is thus not a sin, and the PASSIVE VOICE is an effective means of preserving that impersonality when the scientist writes about scientific experiments. At the same time, however, writers of scientific papers should not be afraid of writing with the active voice and in the first person, if to do so will make their sentences simpler or more logical. After all, people do perform experiments, and there is really nothing wrong with saying so. This is especially the case in papers written by multiple authors; the pronoun *we* is brief, simple, and direct. Sole authors, on the other hand, are wary of the first person singular; the pronoun *I* almost never occurs in scientific papers because it seems to call attention to the author in a way that the pronoun *we* does not. Yet this difference is likely a matter of convention or precedent rather than semantic necessity, and it is possible that scientific writing might seem fresher if single authors were bold enough to use *I* with the active voice now and then instead of the impersonal passive. Thus, either the active voice with the first person pronoun or the passive voice can be recommended, but the alternative means of allegorizing experiments cannot (see PERSONIFICATION; see also PREDICATION, STATEMENT). The presentation of an experiment may be a narrative act, but there is no need for it to be fictional.

Another element of the scientist's impersonal style that bears consideration is the overuse of abstract rather than concrete nouns (see NOUNS AND NOMINALIZATION). Whenever one begins a sentence with an abstract noun, a form of the verb *to be* is likely to follow, along with yet another noun or adjectival construction. Abstractions do not usually do things unless they are personified; they are simply equatable with their attributes or with other abstractions. If a writer begins a sentence with an abstraction, he or she will probably finish it that way, and personal agency will likely seem incidental or be omitted. Consider the following example: *Data sheet distribution was followed by task instruction.* Here the words ending in *-ion* fall like snow that numbs the reader's mind. A passive verb that does not connote any real action links one abstract noun (*distribution*) to another abstract noun (*instruction*), and the concrete nouns *sheet* and *task* are acting simply as adjectives that qualify the abstractions. Meanwhile, the experimenter and the subjects are left out of the sentence. One might begin to improve this sentence by making concrete nouns the subjects of concrete verbs in the passive voice: *After the data sheets were distributed, the subjects were instructed about the task.* Or the concrete verbs could be expressed in the active rather than the passive voice, and their grammatical subjects could be given in the first person: *After we had distributed the data sheets, we instructed the subjects about the task.* Whenever possible, the writer should thus try to choose concrete rather than abstract grammatical subjects; often, one way to do this is to convert the abstract subject into the corresponding concrete verb (*distributed* for *distribution; instructed* for *instruction*). And when people are the agents of the action, personal grammatical subjects will express that action most clearly.

In like manner, one should try to avoid noun modifiers, because they too usually shift the meaning away from the concrete — unless they contribute to specific combinations such as *food cups, nose pokes,* or *goal cages.* Thus, for example, instead of *comparison purposes,* one should write *purposes of comparison,* because the act of comparison is more concrete than the broader, more abstract category *purposes.* For *ease and difficulty judgments,* one should write *judgments of ease and difficulty,* because the latter stresses the concrete types of judgments rather than the general fact that they are judgments. And for *speaker differences in speech production,* one should write *the different ways in which people speak,* or, simply, *differences in speaking.* Nouns modified by prepositional phrases are usually more vivid and concrete than nouns modified by other nouns; the phrase *speaker differences* suggests that differences are important as an overriding category, whereas the phrase *differences in speaking* suggests that the writer is concerned with actual human speech.

Excessive nominalization represents the jargon that pervades much of the language heard in professional or pseudoprofessional contexts. Its unnecessary abstraction and cumbersome phrasal structures contribute to a generally turgid style, which in turn suggests unnecessarily obscure thought. The writer who prefers nominalizing constructions is the sort who will write *we were cognizant that* instead of *we knew that; our determinations utilized* instead of *we determined that it would be best to use;* or *following tape play* instead of *after we had played the tape.* The only way to avoid this sort of style is to be constantly vigilant against abstract subjects and verbs, against the overuse of the verb *to be,* and against noun modifiers, as well as to attempt to choose briefer, simpler synonyms whenever they are available. If the choice of simpler words means that a revision will have to contain more words than are to be found in the original, this does not necessarily mean that the new version is wordy; on the contrary, it usually means that the simpler words in the revision are clearer and more precise.

For further remarks on style, see also INTERESTING TO NOTE; NOUNS AND NOMINALIZATION; PREDICATION, STATEMENT; and WORDINESS.

subjects. Subjects in experiments can be referred to in various ways:

1. *Subject 1, Subject 2, ...* The uppercase "S" is used here because the word *subject* is followed by a designation that names the particular subject.

2. *The subjects were ...* Here lowercase is used, because the subjects are not named.

3. *The rats were ...* Animals are not "subjects" in the same sense as people are, so sometimes it is preferable to call animals by what they really are—that is, *rats, monkeys,* or, in general, *animals.* Regardless of what one chooses to do in such instances, however, one should be consistent. To shift

unnecessarily among *rats, animals,* and *subjects* within a single paragraph can often yield confusion. One should never resort to this tactic merely as a means of avoiding repetition.

4. S and Ss are no longer commonly used for *subject* and *subjects,* presumably because S is still a standard abbreviation for *stimulus.*

subjunctive. In modern American English, the subjunctive is not used widely, but it does occur in specific contexts. Among the most frequent are clauses that follow statements of suggestion or requirement: *I suggest that you come tomorrow at 5:00; the professor demanded that the students remain quiet during the lecture.* In scientific writing, the subjunctive is therefore common in the presentation of experimental requirements: *The episodic task required that the subject discriminate which of several possible relationships had been judged within the confines of the experimental task; the one constraint in choosing the shorter-duration line was that the duration of the other line be less than 400 msec; we have argued that our cross-modal interference and negative priming effects require that the auditory distractors reach a supramodal level of representation.*[74] Note that in each instance, the subjunctive could also be expressed with the verb *should: should discriminate, should be, should reach.* This is not necessary, although it might be appropriate in British usage. But it would be incorrect to use the indicative instead. In the examples just presented, *discriminated* and *was* cannot take the place of *discriminate* and *be;* and *reach,* although it may have the same form as the present plural indicative, is in fact a true subjunctive.

submit. One can submit to another person's authority, or submit one's decision to someone or to some authority for review; one can submit one's results for analysis (i.e., one submits them to someone, who then uses some procedure to analyze them). Webster's also says that *submit* can be used in the sense of "subject to a regime, condition, or practice," and hence psychologists write of *submitting* results *to* analysis.

Even though the dictionary approves of this usage, however, it is hard not to imagine that when *the results were submitted to a three-way repeated measures ANOVA,* the ANOVA is functioning as if it were a sort of punishment or a court of inquiry, and it is equally hard to imagine that rats were submitted to four test sessions. There are other alternatives, which are at least worth considering: Results can be subjected to an ANOVA perhaps; or better still, ANOVAs can be performed on results and they can certainly reveal or yield effects that are present in the results. As for rats, although unlike human subjects they do not *participate* in sessions, they do *undergo* or perhaps even *receive* them, they are *put through* them, or they are *run* in them.

such that. See SO THAT, SUCH THAT.

support, supportive. *Support* is a concise, straightforward verb, whose meanings vary from the concrete to the abstract. A foundation supports a building, voters support a candidate, and friends or lovers can support one another in a variety of ways that range from the financial to the emotional. *Supportive* is an adjective with a long history, but in daily speech, the phrase *supportive of* is post-1960s psychobabble for the latter of these three relationships: *He is very supportive of me.*

Scientists often turn to being *supportive* too: *The present results are supportive of Smith's predictions.* Here, although the writer is not engaging in psychobabble, it is hard to tell what he or she means. Either *supportive of* is jargon for hedging one's bets—that is, the writer is willing only to say that the results *tend* to support the predictions—or it is part of a vague PREDICATION that should be replaced by the verb *support.* Because some writers do not understand the more tentative semantic nuance of the adjective *supportive,* and because this word is strongly tinged with the muddled connotations of pseudotherapeutic thought, it is probably best to avoid it. Either the present results *support* Smith's predictions, or they *seem, tend,* or *appear to support* them. There is no need to call them *supportive.*

T

tense. When a writer reports a scientific experiment, he or she is speaking to the audience in the present about events that have taken place in the past in the "real" world. The writer is thus a present narrator of past events, which have been brought about for specific theoretical purposes. Thus, the typical scientific paper begins with an introduction or a presentation of an argument; a problem is stated, along with the history of the research that has been done to investigate it. The author or authors may introduce the problem in terms of when it *was* first recognized (past tense). They may then state what past researchers *have done* to investigate the problem, what they *have found,* and what they *have claimed* with regard to it (present perfect tense). Next, the authors will likely outline what they *did* to address the problem themselves (past tense). Finally, they will state what they *expected* (past tense) *would* (future, from the perspective of the past) happen when they *did* the experiment (past tense).

For the most part, these verb tenses are easy to handle and need not be discussed. Yet one of the temporal relationships suggested here does cause disproportionate difficulty: the attempt to express the future from the point of view of the past, especially when one is explaining hypotheses made when the experiment was originally designed. Because descriptions of experiments are present narratives about past events, the subjects, apparatus, stimuli, and procedure are described in the past tense: *The subjects were 24 undergraduate students; the stimuli were presented on a black and white video monitor; the subjects were asked to respond by pressing a microswitch;* and so forth. But the presentation of past hypotheses is another matter, as the following sentence illustrates: *If subjects should reinstate antecedents, they would be able to name a reinstated antecedent faster than a nonreinstated antecedent.* In itself this sentence does not suggest a hypothesis about the future stated from the point of view of the past at all; instead, it suggests a subjunctive idea—namely, that if one thing should happen, another would be the case. Indeed the preceding example can only express the future as viewed from time past if it is put into indirect discourse, thus: *On the basis of the model, we assumed that if subjects should reinstate antecedents, they would be able to name a reinstated antecedent faster than a nonreinstated antecedent.* Because the past tense forms of *shall* and *will* in English are also the forms that are used for the subjunctive, only a preceding statement in the past indicative can clarify their use in expressions of futurity from the point of view of the past.

Although it is awkward to do so, the independent clause that introduces the subordinate clause in indirect discourse can also be put in the passive voice, thus: *It was expected that high imagers would acquire the movements more rapidly and remember them better than would low imagers.*[74] Another alternative, also awkward, is to use a predication with an impersonal noun subject to replace the personal subject in the opening independent clause: *The prediction was that the subjective estimates would regress toward the regression function of the stimuli, due to more exposure to the stimuli.*[75] In both instances, the context of the past is clearly stated, so that there can be no confusion between the modal use of the verb and the future tense.

Since scientific writers generally prefer to avoid personal subjects, and since personal subjects are the primary means of beginning independent clauses that are followed by subordinate clauses in indirect discourse, a peculiar convention has evolved for the presentation of past acts of hypothesis; after setting the scene of the experiment with a statement in the past tense, a writer may shift over to the historical present, which is a form that ordinarily occurs only in colloquial speech. Indeed, the writer may do this even after having resorted to the personal subject:

> *In Experiment 2, we tested whether or not the semantic facilitation effect was constrained by the structure of the sentence. If the language processing system performs semantic analysis on subunits of the sentence determined by the syntactic structure, all context information may not be immediately available to facilitate word processing.*[77]

In the formal English that is written outside the world of scientific experimentation, the preceding example would be considered inconsistent. The first sentence sets the context in the past (*we tested*), but in the second one, the writer turns to the present, when in fact the hypothesis was made in the past too. Although this convention seems to have become widespread, the preceding examples of the use of indirect discourse should show that it is possible to avoid such shifts of tense if one wishes.

Another problem that often arises in reports of experiments involves the sequence of tenses used to describe the presentation of stimuli:

> *Old/new recognition tests require subjects to differentiate between items that were and were not presented during a study phase, whereas source monitoring tests require subjects to differentiate between items that were presented via different sources during a study phase.*[78]

In this example, the authors are writing in the present about what is done in certain types of tests. They therefore begin their description in the present tense (*tests require*), and the infinitive *to differentiate* implies that the subjects' actions are being described in the present tense too (this infinitive could, for example, be replaced with the present subjunctive: *tests require that the subjects differentiate*). But when the authors proceed to narrate the sequence of events that the subjects experience during testing, they shift ungrammatically to the past. Note that if the subjects are taking a test, they *are presented* with certain stimuli. They then *respond* to those stimuli. When the subjects thus *respond,* they *are responding* to stimuli that *have been presented* in the past, but whose effect is still felt in the present. If one begins to narrate the preceding events from the point of view of the present, they can only be described appropriately in the present tense, and whenever one is using the present tense to write of past actions whose effect is still felt in the present, one must use the present perfect tense in English, not the simple past. The use of the past tense suggests a remote temporal distance, as if an action's effect is not still felt in the present, which is impossible in the case of a stimulus to which a subject is required to respond. It would be possible to put the entire narration from the point of view of the past of course, but then one would have to use the past perfect to indicate events that ocurred prior to the past itself: *On the recognition test, the subjects were required to differentiate between items that had and had not been presented during a study phase.* Note, however, that this changes the meaning: Whereas in the example above, the authors are writing generally of certain kinds of tests, whose nature may be located in a kind of universal present, in the example set in the past, the test has become a specific, real event. A particular test, rather than that test as a type, has thus been described.

Why that which subjects *have experienced* is ever referred to as what they "experienced" remains a mystery, but this semantic substitution occurs frequently enough to be a part of the experimental scientist's jargon. This makes it no less ungrammatical, however, and it should be avoided.

tense, present continuous. See -ING WORDS.

terms, consistency of. One of the best services that a writer can perform in preparing a paper is to check to see that specific terms are rendered in the same manner throughout the text. This is especially important when segments of papers have been written by different authors; often in such cases, one author will use one version of a term, whereas another will use a diferent version. Whenever this is likely to have occurred, one of the authors should take on the final task of editing for consistency.

For example, if a key term in a paper is *paired-pulse facilitation*, it should not also be referred to as *pair-pulse facilitation*. Nor should one waver between *conditioned* and *conditional responses* or *reaction times* and *response times*. No one should fear repetition here; it is better to repeat a term than to be imprecise because of a desire for stylistic variety. Likewise, one should resist the temptation to shorten such terms by dropping words out. *Paired facilitation* is not the same thing as *paired-pulse facilitation*. Likewise, a *limited-capacity parallel model* is not at all a *limited parallel model*, much less a *limited model*, just as a *bilateral symmetry detection model* is not a *bilateral symmetry model* or a *bilateral model*. As words are removed from such expressions, the terms begin to take on new meanings; in the most compressed versions, the terms become strange. The author who is bothered by the frequent repetition of such terms should choose abbreviations instead, if it seems helpful to do so.

that, conjunction. *That* used as a conjunction to introduce clauses should never be left out of written discourse, regardless of what one may often do in daily speech. Therefore, in the following sentences, the bracketed material should be included:

We suggest [that] these processes would seldom be used.

They found [that] a decrement occurred.

A repeated measures ANOVA confirmed [that] the effect of deprivation was not significant.

In all three examples, if the bracketed *that* were absent, the reader would be likely to misconstrue the word that followed the verb. After the phrase *these processes* in the first sentence, one might expect a construction with *as* or *to be*. In the second sentence, the reader would at first assume that the *decrement* was *found*. And in the third, the reader would similarly construe that the *effect* was *confirmed*. One would have to read each sentence twice to get it right. If, on the other hand, the conjunction *that* is included, there can be no ambiguity upon the first reading of each sentence.

that vs. which. See WHICH.

the. *The* is the definite article. In the most general sense, this means that it is used before a noun that has already been introduced or defined in a given context. If one writes that *the rat was placed in the startbox*, the reader knows what rat is being talked about—not necessarily which particular rat, although this might indeed be the case, but one of *the rats* that have already been mentioned because they were used as subjects in the experiment under discussion. If one says that *a rat was placed in the startbox*, one is speaking more generally, referring to any rat; it could even have been a rat that was *not* one of the subjects. Thus *a* or *an* is called the *indefinite*, as opposed to the *definite*, article. (See also EACH VS. A, AN, OR THE.)

Many scientific writers try never to use the definite article in instances like that just discussed: (a) *Prior to each session, rats were removed from their home cages.* (b) *During each trial, subjects sat in sound-attenuated booths.* (c) *Testing of subjects began on Day 1 following practice trials.* In the English commonly spoken or written outside the scientific context, on the other hand, regardless of the level of style, the definite article would be used in all of these cases: (a) *Prior to each session, the rats were removed from their home cages.* (b) *During each trial, the subjects sat in sound-attenuated booths.* (c) *The testing of the subjects began on Day 1 following practice trials.*

We must therefore ask why the scientific writer would likely differ with the ordinary speaker or writer of English in each of these instances. There are several answers to this question. First, scientific writers strive to present the bare facts to the best of their ability, so they tend to develop a style in which supposedly superfluous words are pruned to a minimum. From such a vantage, the word *the* is certainly superfluous in many cases and can be done away with. Second, the lack of the definite article lends a uniformity to the description of the subjects and the testing, which in turn serves as a stylistic means of confirming that the scientist is always looking for general principles that can account for replicable phenomena. Third, the omission of the definite article creates a professional tone, which confers covert prestige on the writer as part of a knowledgeable scientific elite. Fourth, the lack of the definite article contributes indirectly to the impersonal tone that has always been a hallmark of scientific style; because universal principles of behavioral experience are being sought, the particularizing tendency of the personal is studiously avoided. Fifth, as any native speaker of a foreign language will readily admit when learning English for the first time, it is easier to create sentences without the definite article than it is to figure out when the definite article should be used in English and when it should not.

Despite such motivations or justifications, there is good reason to include the definite article, just as one does in ordinary speech. First, it is unnatural to leave it out. Second, its omission is depersonalizing and therefore demeaning to subjects, particular human ones. Third, it adds concreteness and vividness to the language. We do not use the definite article for general concepts in English as one does in French or German; we use it to be precise and specific. And precision is what the scientist ought to strive for, in language as well as in mathematics. To the writer who may object that this implies an overuse of the word *the,* thereby cluttering the page with excess verbiage, it must be stressed that only in scientific writing and in the obfuscating jargons of governmental bureaucracies is the lack of the definite article a norm; and that in this instance the implicit recommendation of common usage among all levels of good style, ranging from street slang to formal essayistic prose, should be allowed to prevail. Any sensitive reader, on encountering the three sentences given above, will ask, respectively: (a) What rats? The rats that were the subjects in this experiment? (b) What subjects? The subjects in the present experiment? (c) What testing and what subjects? Those in the present experiment? No reader should have to ask such questions. That anyone should ask them at all means that the word *the,* when used correctly, is not at all obtrusive; its absence is. (See also BRAIN.).

there is, there are. Frequently sentences or clauses beginning with *there is, there are,* or *there have been* can be boiled down to fewer words. This represents a particular instance of WORDINESS, in which the adverb *there* occupies what should be the position of the grammatical subject in the sentence, and the true subject is delayed until it follows the verb *is* or *are.* To remedy the following examples, *there is* and *there are* must be removed, and the delayed subject must be made the subject before the verb:

Wordy: *Thus, there is now a view emerging that…*
Better: *Thus, the view now emerging is that…*
Best: *Thus, the emerging view is that…*

Wordy: *There have, however, been a small number of longitudinal studies which have established that…*[79]
Better: *However, a small number of longitudinal studies have established that…*

Careful comparison of these two sets of examples shows that the removal of *there is* or *there are* also permits the useful excision of other unnecessary verbiage.

this latter, the latter. See LATTER, THE.

to, in order. See PURPOSE, CONSTRUCTION OF.

to, lexical decisions to, ERPs to, etc. See STIMULUS–RE-SPONSE LANGUAGE.

transitional words and phrases. Because success in writing depends on the logical, lucid, and fluent development of the writer's thoughts on a given subject, all handbooks on grammar and style include chapters or sections on transitions and transitional expressions. Such discussions are always accompanied by lists of words, called *conjunctive adverbs,* and transitional phrases that one can use to link clauses or sentences together. Examples of conjunctive adverbs include *also, furthermore, hence, however, indeed, moreover, nevertheless, nonetheless, rather, still, then, therefore,* and *thus;* examples of transitional phrases include *as a result, at the same time, in fact, in other words, on the contrary, on the other hand,* and so forth. Such words and phrases are invaluable. But in the hands of the unsure writer, they can easily become the wooden signs of stylistic immaturity. If within a single paragraph, for example, every sentence but the first opens with a transitional expression followed by a comma, it will seem as if every sentence was originally written on a separate note card, and the transitions, marking the divisions, will obtrusively detract from the reader's apprehension of the thoughts that the transitions are intended to link. The following passage, although acceptable, illustrates this tendency:

> *However, there are problems with the foregoing interpretation. For instance, Jacoby (1983) has reported that some variables produce common effects on recognition memory and the word repetition effect in tachistoscopic word identification (although the relative magnitudes of any changes may differ). Thus, increasing the proportion of words that are in both the initial and the test lists aids recognition memory (Jacoby, 1972) and produces a larger word repetition effect on tachistoscopic identification (Jacoby, 1983). Also, although the word repetition effect on tachistoscopic report and lexical decision is strikingly persistent, some decreases are found over retention intervals which produce decreases in recognition memory (Jacoby, 1983; see also Ratcliff, Hockley, & McKoon,*

1985; Scarborough et al., 1977).[80]

A careful reading of the foregoing should reveal that of the four transitional words or expressions used, only the last is necessary. The first sentence clearly states a contrast with the interpretation in the preceding paragraph, so *however* is superfluous. The second sentence at once gives one of the problems mentioned in the first sentence, so the phrase *for instance* is not necessary either. The third sentence presents one of the variables mentioned in the second sentence, so the adverb *thus* is likewise superfluous. The last sentence, however, which begins with *although,* does not introduce another such variable; instead it presents another problem for the previously mentioned interpretation. The word *also* therefore clarifies the fourth sentence's relation to the rest. Had the writers thought more carefully about the meaning of each sentence, they might have realized that the transitions were implicitly present already, so that the additional rhetorical instructions could have been dispensed with. The overabundance of such transitions in scientific writing suggests that writers are afraid to let their thoughts speak for themselves, perhaps because of prior exposure to unnecessarily pedantic English teachers.

When one does use conjunctive adverbs or transitional phrases, however, one should remember the following principles: (a) The conjunctive adverb does not need to begin a sentence. It may be located not only in the initial position, but also after any complete unit of thought: *However, the rats in the 12-mg ketamine group displayed total avoidance of saccharin. At the time of surgery, however, the body weights of the rats were lower. The damage to the hippocampus was different from that described previously, however.* When the adverb occurs later in the sentence, it is less obtrusive, and the continuity of the writer's thought is often smoother. (b) When the conjunctive adverb or transitional phrase joins independent clauses, the clauses are separated by a semicolon, not a comma. If the semicolon follows the conjunctive adverb, the adverb suggests a contrast with the preceding sentence; if the semicolon precedes the adverb, the adverb suggests a contrast between the two clauses that it links (See under COMMAS, especially *Commas and coordination: Compound sentences and compound verbs or predicates; Commas with for example or that is; Commas with transitional words.* See also COORDINATION and FOR EXAMPLE.)

U, V

uppercase. See LOWERCASE, UPPERCASE. See also any good dictionary.

use, using. The verb *to use* is one of the most *overused* words *used* by *users* of English for professional *uses.* Perhaps owing to this ubiquity, *to use* can be misused in a variety of ways. Thus, at the annual meeting of the Society for Computers in Psychology in 1984, Thomas T. Hewett of Drexel University presented a paper on "Teaching students to model neural circuits and neural networks using an electronic spreadsheet simulator."[81] Here, *using* appears at first to be a participle, and participles modify nouns. But what in the title is using the spreadsheet simulator? Because *using* follows the noun *networks,* it would ordinarily be construed as modifying that word. But networks are not using the simulator. The reader must therefore backtrack until he or she finds the next most likely word or group of words that *using* could modify. These words may be found in the implied statement that the *students are modeling the network;* given this interpretation, the title must mean that the students are modeling the network *by using* the simulator. Now *using* is no longer a participle but a gerund acting as the object of the preposition *by.* But it is still more likely that the instructor is using the spreadsheet simulator to teach the students, even though the instructor is not mentioned in the title. It will do no good to argue that the instructor is understood to be teaching the students and using the simulator to do it, for the grammar of the title suggests that *using,* unlike *teaching,* does not refer to the action of the understood instructor at all. And the fact that *using* may here be construed as either a gerund or a participle, depending on how one interprets the title, shows that the grammatical function of this word has been made ambiguous.

I dwell on this example at length because it typifies a current trend in style, whereby the vague word *using* is allowed to stand for other more precise words and to take on the functions of various parts of speech. It is thus common to read of *findings using a word-recognition paradigm* instead of *findings obtained in [with] a word-recognition paradigm;* of *subjects* who *smelled the stimuli using an odorant delivery system* when in fact the stimuli *were delivered* by such a system; of *the results in a study using a cued recall task* instead of *the results of the cued recall task;* of *the limiting factor using this technique* instead of *the limitation of this technique;* and so forth. In every one of these instances, the participle *using* functions as an illogical modifier, for findings do not use paradigms; stimuli do not use delivery systems, nor do subjects use such systems to smell stimuli either; neither results nor studies use tasks; and factors do not use techniques.

Perhaps the most common class of such errors is the prepositional application of *using,* which is especially peculiar because participles are seldom applied in this manner. Thus, a writer will say that *the computer is controlled using the keyboard* when in fact it is simply controlled *with* the keyboard. Or again, the reader will be told that *subjects were tested using the procedure from Experiment 1,* when in fact the *subjects were tested with [according to] the procedure from Experiment 1.* In such instances, whenever a true preposition can be substituted for *using,* that preposition should be employed instead. Usually it will turn out to be the preposition *with.*

The simplest solution to these grammatical and semantic dilemmas is to avoid forms of the verb *to use* as often as possible; anyone who can do so will then manage to use it with normal frequency. The writer should also remember that studies, experiments, procedures, tasks, and trials do not *use* subjects, materials, apparatus, or anything else; researchers use these things, in their studies, experiments, procedures, tasks, and trials. (See PREDICATION, STATEMENT; see also PERSONIFICATION.)

versus. *Versus* should be spelled out when it does not occur inside parentheses. Within parentheses, it should be abbreviated *vs.* (In older issues of some journals, however, *vs* can be found without the period; when it occurs thus in titles of published works, it should be reproduced that way in entries on reference lists.)

Versus should not be used in place of *as opposed to, in opposition to, rather than,* or *with* when one is making a comparison. Economy of style is not a good enough reason for one to write: *The scores were significantly higher for focused versus divided attention.* Here are some alternatives:

> *The scores were significantly higher for focused, as opposed to divided, attention.*

> *The scores were significantly higher for focused, rather than divided, attention.*

> *The scores were significantly higher for focused than they were for divided attention.*

The reader may wonder what is wrong with the word *versus* in the first sentence. It is that *versus* is not semantically part of a comparative construction. Literally, if one says that scores were *higher for focused versus divided attention,* a construction introduced by the word *than,* or the phrase *as opposed to,* is still expected to follow *attention.* (See also ABBREVIATIONS, LATIN.)

via. This word is jargon for other prepositions or prepositional constructions. Thus, *via telephone* means *on the tele-*

phone; reaction times recorded via a voice key are reaction times recorded *with the use of a voice key; stimuli presented via a computer monitor* are stimuli presented *on a computer monitor.* Probably no use of *via* lacks a prepositional counterpart. As is the case with USING, when a single word thus corresponds to many other words that are more vivid or precise, it is usually better to use one of those words than it is to use the all-purpose alternative.

viz. This now uncommon abbreviation is short for the Latin *videlicet,* meaning "it is easy to see" or "one may or can see." In English usage, it is taken to mean "namely." It should be used only inside parentheses; outside the parentheses, one should use its English translation. (See also ABBREVIATIONS, LATIN.)

W

where. The primary meaning of the word *where* involves reference to spatial motion or location: *That is the lab where she does her research.* (Here, *where* is plainly a substitute for *in which.*) A relatively specialized use of *where* occurs in mathematics, which allows the use of *where* to introduce explanations: $y = f(x)$, where y is a dependent variable and x is an independent variable, such that for every x there is one and only one value of y. It is often awkward, however, to use *where* for abstract relationships that are only metaphorically spatial, unless the language sanctions such instances as idioms. No matter how conventional it may seem to some writers, to others it will seem peculiar to write of *a condition where subjects had 5 sec of contextual exposure, an experiment where subjects made lexical decisions,* or *a study where the presentation of suffixes has been manipulated.* Conditions, experiments, and studies are not in any way spatial phenomena. It is of course true that in every one of these examples, *in which* could be substituted for *where;* but this is because it is idiomatically correct to refer to what goes on *in conditions, in experiments,* and *in studies.* The use of *in which* in the three examples given above thus reflects the idiomatic usage that is permitted with three particular nouns; it does not in any way suggest the sort of spatial relationship that would warrant the use of *where* instead.

which. *Which* is particularly noteworthy as a relative pronoun whose use is surrounded by some controversy. Thus, for example, a highly respected scientist from the United Kingdom was once offended by an American editor's frequent changing of *which* to *that* in her manuscript; Americans, she asserted, simply do not understand the word *which* at all. The issue involved the distinction between the "restrictive" and the "nonrestrictive" uses of words such as *which, that,* and *who:* many American writers and editors differentiate between *that* and *which* by reserving *which* solely for the nonrestrictive meaning of the relative pronoun. *That,* on the other hand, is never at issue here, for it is always restrictive.[82] This difference may be illustrated best through examples; it will be instructive, however, to begin with the pronoun *who:*

> The subjects, <u>who were between 18 and 22 years of age</u>, were tested on the 2nd and 3rd days.

> The subjects <u>who were between 18 and 22 years of age</u> were tested on the 2nd and 3rd days.

The underlined segments are both relative clauses. The first one is said to be "nonrestrictive" and is set off by commas; the second is said to be "restrictive" and is not thus demarcated. The former term reflects the fact that the nonrestrictive relative clause does not restrict or limit the meaning of the noun *(subjects)* to which it refers; in the first sentence, all of the subjects are between 18 and 22 years old, and no other subjects are implied. But in the second sentence, it is implied that there were other subjects as well, and that only those who were between 18 and 22 were tested on Days 2 and 3. Thus, in the second sentence, the relative clause is said to be "restrictive," because it restricts or limits the meaning of the noun *subjects*.

If we apply the same rule to the distinction between *which* and *that*, the former, when it is a relative pronoun, will always be set off by commas because it is nonrestrictive, and the latter, when it is acting as a relative pronoun, will not, because it is always restrictive. A corollary follows: Whenever *which* might be used restrictively, it should be replaced with *that*. Here are some examples.

That, restrictive:
To address this apparent paradox, we took animals that were stressed by chronic daily exposure to one stressor (homotypic condition) and exposed them to a novel stressor (heterotypic condition).[83]

In this instance, only the animals that were thus stressed were exposed to the novel stressor; they are implicitly differentiated from other animals that were not thus stressed.

Which, nonrestrictive:
These patterns, which were presented at equal intensities and were relatively simple, lessened the likelihood that masking would interfere with judgments of temporal order.

In this example, only one set of patterns is referred to; *which*, set off by a comma, is used, because the relative clause does not restrict the meaning of *patterns* by contrasting them with other patterns.

Which, nonrestrictive:
The PSE, which was estimated in the same manner as in the previous experiment, was 67.9 mm.[84]

Here there is of course only one PSE; *which* is therefore appropriate because it does not define the PSE restrictively in relation to other PSEs. Had the authors chosen *that* without the comma instead, and written the following sentence—

The PSE that was estimated in the same manner as in the previous experiment was 67.9 mm

—it would mean that there were still other PSEs besides the one mentioned here.

Consider now the following sentence:

Brewster and Leon (1980) described a behavior pattern in the infant rat, which enables the mother to transport the pup efficiently from one location to another.[85]

Here the author has chosen the nonrestrictive form of the relative pronoun, set off by commas. Yet there are many behavior patterns in the infant rat, and in this instance one of them is being isolated from all the rest. Therefore, the relative clause, in defining that particular pattern of behavior, restricts the meaning of the term (*behavior pattern*) to which it refers. The sentence should have been written or edited thus:

Brewster and Leon (1980) described a behavior pattern in the infant rat that enables the mother to transport the pup efficiently from one location to another.

There remains the question of whether it is ever acceptable to use *which* instead of *that* in the restrictive sense. In fact it is, but this practice can sometimes blur the distinction between the restrictive and nonrestrictive usages given above. The writer who wishes to use *which* for the restrictive meaning would be well advised to do so in the interests of style rather than arbitrariness. If more than one *that* occurs in proximity, thereby causing repetition, then perhaps *which* will do for one of them; otherwise the distinction between *which* and *that* should be preserved. (See also THAT, CONJUNCTION.)

while. Although dictionaries generally accept the use of *while* to mean "although," many editors of scientific writing do not. Scientific experiments often involve the manipulation or measurement of units or durations of time as part of the investigation of physical and behavioral phenomena, and the subjects in scientific experiments are tested according to temporal schedules. This means that in presenting experiments, one will almost always discuss units of time of some sort. In such a context, the word *while* can easily become ambiguous. If *while* is used to mean "although," it can be misconstrued as connoting simultaneity when in fact the writer is making a logical concession:

> *These results suggest that while the retarded subjects could discriminate the spatial location of the form, they perceived it as having poorly defined contours.*

Here, *while* seems to be a temporal conjunction, but that is not what the author intends. To express the author's meaning without any ambiguity, the sentence should read:

> *These results suggest that although the retarded subjects could discriminate the spatial location of the form, they perceived it as having poorly defined contours.*

Thus, even though it is acceptable to use *while* to mean "although," for the sake of clarity it is often best not to do so. In the context of the scientific paper, if *while* could always signify temporal relationships and if *although* could always signify adverbial concessions, no ambiguity would ever arise in the use of these words. (See also AS.)

within group(s). See BETWEEN GROUP, WITHIN GROUP...

within subjects. See BETWEEN SUBJECT[S], WITHIN SUBJECTS...

wordiness. A concise, concrete, direct style is preferable to any other, unless one is striving for a particular aesthetic effect that calls for something else. This means that one should always try to prune one's writing, cutting away excess verbiage and converting nominalized abstractions into concrete subjects and verbs whenever possible.

The following examples should speak for themselves; samples of wordiness speak louder than rules.

Wordy: *a great deal of*
Better: *much*

Wordy: *these types of responses*
Better: *such responses*

Wordy: *despite the fact that*
Better: *even though*

Wordy: *the experimental subjects, 3 cebus monkeys,…*
Better: *the subjects, 3 cebus monkeys,…*

Wordy: *the hypothesis which states that*
Better: *the hypothesis that*

Wordy: *an issue that is clear is that*
Better: *it is clear that*

Wordy: *there is much evidence to suggest that*
Better: *much evidence suggests that*

Wordy: *there is not much knowledge concerning*
Better: *not much is known about*

Wordy: *there is much variation in x*
Better: *x displays much variation; x varies considerably*

Wordy: *the approach of using*
Better: *the use of*
Still better, if appropriate: *to use*

Wordy: *the method that we previously used*
Better: *our previous method*

Wordy: *intervals of long duration*
Better: *long intervals*

Wordy: *the responses shown by rats*
Better: *the responses of rats*
Still better: *the rats' responses*

Wordy: *during the course of object perception*
Better: *during object perception*

Wordy: *with a view toward widening the scope of*
Better: *to widen the scope of*
Still better, if appropriate: *to widen*

Wordy: *this constant is always negatively signed*
Better: *this constant is always negative*

Wordy: *They performed an experiment in which subjects were
          required to...*
Better: *They required subjects to...*

Wordy: *According to this hypothesis, the subject is purported
          to have...*
Better: *According to this hypothesis, the subject has...*

Wordy: *It was reasoned that...*
Better: *We reasoned that...*

Wordy: *Subjects made judgments regarding the similarity
          of...*
Better: *Subjects judged the similarity of...*

Wordy: *We were faced with the task of measuring...*
Better: *We had to measure...*

Wordy: *This was accomplished with the use of...*
Better: *This was done with...*

Wordy: *Switching output can be accomplished by...*
Better: *One can switch the output by...*

Wordy: *.45° in width*
Better: *.45° wide*

Wordy: *.40° and .56° in the horizontal and vertical directions*
Better: *.40° horizontally and .56° vertically*

Wordy: *Each letter in the stimulus display subtended a horizontal visual angle of .30 degrees and a vertical visual angle of .60 degrees.*
Better: *Each letter was .30° wide and .60° high.*

Wordy: *The saccades did not differ in their accuracy or velocity characteristics.*
Better: *The saccades did not differ in accuracy or velocity.*

Wordy: *Evidence of bimodality cannot be discerned through visual inspection of the histograms.*
Better: *The histograms reveal no visual evidence for bimodality.*

Wordy: *There have, however, been a small number of longitudinal studies which have established that measures of phonological short-term memory and phonological awareness skills either before reading or as children begin reading tuition are good predictors of subsequent reading success.*[86]
Better: *However, in a few longitudinal studies, measures of phonological short-term memory and phonological awareness in children who either do not yet or are just beginning to read have predicted later reading success as well.*

Endnotes

[1]In this entry, when two abbreviations occur, the first is that preferred by the American Psychological Association, the second that preferred by the Psychonomic Society.

[2]Strictly speaking, the hyphen in 1–5 days and 22°–24° C is not a hyphen per se but an en-dash, which is usually reserved for typesetting ranges of numbers or other abbreviations such as S–R (for stimulus–response). Writers of manuscripts seldom need to indicate this distinction; it is the copy editor's responsibility.

[3]From D.J. Finlay and P.C. Dodwell (1987). Speed of apparent motion and the wagon-wheel effect. *Perception & Psychophysics, 41*, 32.

[4]These abbreviations are culled from papers edited by the staff at the publications office of the Psychonomic Society.

[5]R.G. Crowder and J. Morton (1969). Precategorical acoustic storage (PAS). *Perception & Psychophysics, 5*, 365–373.

[6]From D.C. Geary, K.F. Widaman, and T.D. Little (1986). Cognitive addition and multiplication: Evidence for a single memory network. *Memory & Cognition, 14*, 478.

[7]From K. Jordan and J. Haleblian (1988). Orientation specificity of length assimilation and contrast. *Perception & Psychophysics, 43*, 452.

[8]From R.L. Port, A.G. Romano, and M.M. Patterson (1986). Stimulus duration discrimination in the rabbit: Effects of hippocampectomy on discrimination and reversal learning. *Physiological Psychology, 14*, 125.

[9]From T. Garrick, T.R. Minor, S. Bauck, H. Weiner, and P. Guth (1989). Predictable and unpredictable shock stimulates gastric contractility and causes mucosal injury in rats. *Behavioral Neuroscience, 103*, 126.

[10]From J.R. Anderson and L.M. Reder (1987). Effects of number of facts studied on recognition versus sensibility judgments. *Journal of Experimental Psychology: Learning, Memory, and Cognition, 13*, 356.

[11]From R.D. Melara and L.E. Marks (1990). HARD and SOFT interacting dimensions: Differential effects of dual context on classification. *Perception & Psychophysics, 47*, 321.

[12]From T.F. Oltmans (1987). Current progress in schizophrenia research. *Contemporary Psychology, 32*, 315.

[13]From P.T. Hertel and T.S. Hardin (1990). Remembering with and without awareness in a depressed mood: Evidence of deficits in initiative.

Journal of Experimental Psychology: General, 119, 55.

[14]From N.G. Kanwisher and M.C. Potter (1990). Repetition blindness: Levels of processing. *Journal of Experimental Psychology: Human Perception and Performance, 16,* 30.

[15]From S. Grossberg (1987). Cortical dynamics of three-dimensional form, color, and brightness perception: I. Monocular theory. *Perception & Psychophysics, 41,* 88.

[16]From J.S. Cohen, J. Grassi, and P. Dowson (1988). The role of within-trial location of the retention interval in rats' delayed conditional discrimination performance. *Animal Learning & Behavior, 16,* 42.

[17]From M.D. Zeiler (1991). Ecological influences on timing. *Journal of Experimental Psychology: Animal Behavior Processes, 17,* 17.

[18]For more detailed discussions, the reader should consult the *Chicago Manual of Style* and *Words into Type.*

[19]P. Panula, M.S. Airaksinen, U. Pirvola, and E. Kotilainen (1990). A histamine-containing neuronal system in human brain. *Neuroscience, 34,* 131.

[20]From A.F. Kramer and A. Jacobson (1991). Perceptual organization and focused attention: The role of objects and proximity in visual processing. *Perception & Psychophysics, 50,* 269.

[21]From M.E. Bouton and D. Swartzentruber (1989). Slow reacquisition following extinction: Context, encoding, and retrieval mechanisms. *Journal of Experimental Psychology: Animal Behavior Processes, 15,* 45.

[22]From H. Ono and M.J. Steinbach (1990). Monocular stereopsis with and without head movement. *Perception & Psychophysics, 48,* 183.

[23]From W.R. Uttal (1990). On some two-way barriers between models and mechanisms. *Perception & Psychophysics, 48,* 188.

[24]From G.C. Rikard-Bell, I. Törk, C. Sullivan, and T. Scheibner (1990). Distribution of substance P-like immunoreactive fibres and terminals in the medulla oblongata of the human infant. *Neuroscience, 34,* 133.

[25]From D.L. King (1990). A large rectangle delays the perception of a separate small rectangle. *Perception & Psychophysics, 47,* 369.

[26]From W.V. Edhouse and K. G. White (1988). Sources of proactive interference in animal memory. *Journal of Experimental Psychology: Animal Behavior Processes, 14,* 67.

[27]From R.D. Melara and L.E. Marks (1990). Interaction among auditory dimensions: Timbre, pitch, and loudness. *Perception & Psychophysics, 48,* 171.

[28]From B. Hughes, W. Epstein, S. Schneider, and A. Dudock (1990). An asymmetry in transmodal perceptual learning. *Perception & Psychophysics, 48,* 148.

[29]From C.L. Heinbuck and W.A. Hershberger (1989). Development of visual attention: A stereoscopic view. *Perception & Psychophysics, 45,* 406.

[30]From L.L. Jacoby and C.A.G. Hayman (1987). Specific visual transfer in word identification. *Journal of Experimental Psychology: Learning, Memory,*

and Cognition, 13, 458.

[31]From P. Barone, S.A. Parashos, V. Palma, C. Marin, G. Campanella, and T.N. Chase (1990). Dopamine D1 receptor modulation of pilocarpine-induced convulsions. *Neuroscience, 34,* 210.

[32]From J.R. Ison and L.A. Pinckney (1990). Inhibition of the cutaneous eyeblink reflex by unilateral and bilateral acoustic input: The persistence of contralateral antagonism in auditory processing. *Perception & Psychophysics, 47,* 340.

[33]From R.W. Richards and D.B. Richardson (1991). Delayed reinforcement: Effect of a brief signal on behavior maintained by a variable-ratio schedule. *Bulletin of the Psychonomic Society, 29,* 543.

[34]From H.L. Roitblat and H.E. Hartley (1988). Spatial delayed matching-to-sample performance by rats: Learning, memory, and proactive interference. *Journal of Experimental Psychology: Animal Behavior Processes, 14,* 77.

[35]From H. Pashler (1987). Target-distractor discriminability in visual search. *Perception & Psychophysics, 41,* 290.

[36]From W.R. Uttal (1990). On some two-way barriers between models and mechanisms. *Perception & Psychophysics, 48,* 189.

[37]From R.D. Melara and L.E. Marks (1990). Interaction among auditory dimensions: Timbre, pitch, and loudness. *Perception & Psychophysics, 48,* 171.

[38]From W.R. Uttal (1990). On some two-way barriers between models and mechanisms. *Perception & Psychophysics, 48,* 189.

[39]From S. Edwards and R. Stevens (1991). Effects of the peripheral 5-HT2 antagonist xylamidine on consummatory behaviors. *Psychobiology, 19,* 244.

[40]From P. Wenderoth and T. O'Connor (1987). Outline- and solid-angle orientation illusions have different determinants. *Perception & Psychophysics, 41,* 47.

[41]From J.D. St. James (1990). Observations on the microstructure of response conflict. *Perception & Psychophysics, 48,* 522.

[42]From G.W. Heiman, R.J. Leo, G. Leighbody, and K. Bowler (1986). Word intelligibility decrements and the comprehension of time-compressed speech. *Perception & Psychophysics, 40,* 409.

[43]From P.L. Emerson (1986). Observations on maximum-likelihood and Bayesian methods of forced-choice sequential threshold estimation. *Perception & Psychophysics, 39,* 153.

[44]From M.A. Heller (1992). The effect of orientation on tactual braille recognition: Optimal touching positions. *Perception & Psychophysics, 52,* 550.

[45]In the February 1990 issue of the *Journal of Experimental Psychology: Human Perception and Performance,* for example, one will find on page 66 the following left-hand column heading: "The Neighborhood-Frequency Effect." Yet two paragraphs down, the same term is introduced (in italics)

as the "neighborhood frequency effect." Remarkably, in the right-hand column on the same page, it is also called the "neighborhood/frequency effect." Again in the same issue, on page 135, the title of an article refers to "Focused Attention Tasks," but the abstract on the same page contains the phrase "focused- and divided-attention paradigms." Whether such variety owes to the authors or to the editors is hard to tell.

[46]From S. Yantis and J. Jonides (1990). Abrupt visual onsets and selective attention: Voluntary versus automatic allocation. *Journal of Experimental Psychology: Human Perception and Performance, 16,* 126.

[47]From D. Jared and M.S. Seidenberg (1990). Naming multisyllabic words. *Journal of Experimental Psychology: Human Perception and Performance, 16,* 94.

[48]From W. Hershberger (1987). Saccadic eye movements and the perception of visual direction. *Perception & Psychophysics, 41,* 42.

[49]From J. Jonides and M. Naveh-Benjamin (1987). Estimating frequency of occurrence. *Journal of Experimental Psychology: Learning, Memory, and Cognition, 13,* 232.

[50]From J.M. Loomis (1990). A model of character recognition and legibility. *Journal of Experimental Psychology: Human Perception and Performance, 16,* 112.

[51]From S. Yantis and J.C. Johnston (1990). On the locus of visual selection: Evidence from focused attention tasks. *Journal of Experimental Psychology: Human Perception and Performance, 16,* 144.

[52]A. Santi and M. Mielke (1991). Flexible coding of temporal information by pigeons: Event durations as remember and forget cues for temporal samples. *Animal Learning & Behavior, 19,* 171–176.

[53]From S.J. Lederman, R.L. Klatzky, C. Chataway, and C.D. Summers (1990). Visual mediation and the haptic recognition of two-dimensional pictures of common objects. *Perception & Psychophysics, 47,* 61.

[54]From R.W. Frick (1987). The homogeneity effect in counting. *Perception & Psychophysics, 41,* 8.

[55]From W.K. Estes (1987). Application of a cognitive-distance model to learning in a simulated travel task. *Journal of Experimental Psychology: Learning, Memory, and Cognition, 13,* 380.

[56]From D.J. Finlay and P.C. Dodwell (1987). Speed of apparent motion and the wagon-wheel effect. *Perception & Psychophysics, 41,* 31.

[57]From J. Morrow-Tesch and J.J. McGlone (1990). Sensory systems and nipple attachment behavior in neonatal pigs. *Physiology & Behavior, 47,* 1.

[58]From D.L. Schacter, L.A. Cooper, and S.M. Delaney (1990). Implicit memory for unfamiliar objects depends on access to structural descriptions. *Journal of Experimental Psychology: General, 119,* 8.

[59]From M. Remy and J. Emmerton (1989). Behavioral spectral sensitivities of different retinal areas in pigeons. *Behavioral Neuroscience, 103,* 171.

[60]From J. Lovejoy and K. Wallen (1988). Sexually dimorphic behavior in group-housed rhesus monkeys (*Macaca mulatta*) at 1 year of age. *Psy-*

chobiology, 16, 350.

[61]See R. Huddleston (1984). *Introduction to the grammar of English* (pp. 272–298). Cambridge: Cambridge University Press, for a good introduction to pronouns.

[62]From S.S. Stevens and H. Davis (1983). *Hearing: Its psychology and physiology* (p. 310). New York: American Institute of Physics. (Original work published 1938)

[63]From N.F. Johnson, K.R. Pugh, and A.J. Blum (1989). More on the way we "see" letters from words within memory. *Journal of Memory and Language, 28,* 157; in the third sentence, the original reads *is* rather than *was,* which I have silently changed here so that the two purposes would be expressed in the past.

[64]For some examples of how *same* and *different* have been handled in several papers, see R.W. Proctor, T. van Zandt, and H.D. Watson (1990). Effects of background symmetry on *same–different* pattern matching: A compromise-criteria account. *Perception & Psychophysics, 48,* 543–550; W.T. Neill, L. S. Lissner, and J.L. Beck (1990). Negative priming in *same–different* matching: Further evidence for a central locus of inhibition. *Perception & Psychophysics, 48,* 398–400; D.L. King (1988). Strong phenomenal wholes are associated with fast "same" and slow "different" responses and superior overall performance. *Perception & Psychophysics, 43,* 485–493; and L.E. Krueger and P.A. Allen (1987). *Same–different* judgments of foveal and parafoveal letter pairs by older adults. *Perception & Psychophysics, 41,* 329–334. For an analogous, yet different, solution to the use of the terms *hard* and *soft,* see R.D. Melara and L.E. Marks (1990). HARD and SOFT interacting dimensions: Differential effects of dual context on classification. *Perception & Psychophysics, 47,* 307–325.

[65]This and the preceding example are from P.A. Allen and D.J. Madden (1990). Evidence for a parallel input serial analysis model of word processing. *Journal of Experimental Psychology: Human Perception and Performance, 16,* 49.

[66]From S. Goss, C. Hall, E. Buckolz, and G. Fishburne (1986). Imagery ability and the acquisition and retention of movements. *Memory & Cognition, 14,* 469.

[67]From W.T. Neill, L.S. Lissner, and J.L. Beck (1990). Negative priming in *same–different* matching: Further evidence for a central locus of inhibition. *Perception & Psychophysics, 48,* 398.

[68]From S. Yantis and J. Jonides (1990). Abrupt visual onsets and selective attention: Voluntary versus automatic allocation. *Journal of Experimental Psychology: Human Perception and Performance, 16,* 126.

[69]From D. Jared and M.S. Seidenberg (1990). Naming multisyllabic words. *Journal of Experimental Psychology: Human Perception and Performance, 16,* 92.

[70]From E.J. Capaldi and D.J. Miller (1988). Counting in rats: Its functional significance and the independent cognitive processes that constitute

it. *Journal of Experimental Psychology: Animal Behavior Processes, 14,* 4.

[71]From G.W. Humphries, D. Blesner, and P.T. Quinlan (1988). Event perception and the word repetition effect. *Journal of Experimental Psychology: General, 117,* 51.

[72]From R. Ley and K. Long (1988). Distractor similarity effects in tests of discrimination recognition and distractor-free recognition. *Bulletin of the Psychonomic Society, 26,* 408.

[73]The latter example is from M.A. Gluck and G.H. Bower (1990). Component and pattern information in adaptive networks. *Journal of Experimental Psychology: General, 119,* 107.

[74]The three preceding examples are from N.E.A. Kroll and W. Klimesch (1992). Semantic memory: Complexity or connectivity? *Memory & Cognition, 20,* 205; A.M. Glenberg, K.A. Eberhardt, and T.M. Belden (1987). The role of visual interference in producing the long-term modality effect. *Memory & Cognition, 15,* 508; and J. Driver and G.C. Baylis (1993). Cross-modal negative priming and interference in selective attention. *Bulletin of the Psychonomic Society, 31,* 48.

[75]From S. Goss, C. Hall, E. Buckolz, and G. Fishburne (1986). Imagery ability and the acquisition and retention of movements. *Memory & Cognition, 14,* 470.

[76]From R.A. Malmi (1986). Intuitive covariation estimation. *Memory & Cognition, 14,* 503.

[77]From P. Carroll and M.L. Slowiaczek (1986). Constraints on semantic priming in reading: A fixation time analysis. *Memory & Cognition, 14,* 511.

[78]From D.S. Lindsay and M.K. Johnson (1991). Recognition memory and source monitoring. *Bulletin of the Psychonomic Society, 29,* 203.

[79]From S.E. Gathercole and A.D. Baddeley (1989). Evaluation of the role of phonological STM in the development of vocabulary in children: A longitudinal study. *Journal of Memory and Language, 28,* 201.

[80]G.W. Humphreys, D. Besner, and P.T. Quinlan (1988). Event perception and the word repetition effect. *Journal of Experimental Psychology: General, 117,* 52.

[81]*Behavior Research Methods, Instruments, & Computers.* (1985). *17,* 339–344.

[82]The word *that* of course has other uses; we are only concerned with the relative pronoun here.

[83]From M. Konarska, R.E. Stewart, and R. McCarty (1990). Habituation of plasma catecholamine responses to chronic intermittent restraint stress. *Psychobiology, 18,* 33.

[84]From K. Jordan and J. Haleblian (1988). Orientation specificity of length assimilation and contrast. *Perception & Psychophysics, 43,* 450.

[85]From C. Wilson (1988). The effects of apomorphine and lithium chloride on the "transport response" in white rats. *Bulletin of the Psychonomic Society, 26,* 452.

[86]From S.E. Gathercole and A.D. Baddeley (1989). Evaluation of the role

of phonological STM in the development of vocabulary in children: A longitudinal study. *Journal of Memory and Language, 28,* 201.

Selected Bibliography

The following list includes college English handbooks, which are good for refreshing one's mind about grammatical terms and categories, guides to usage, style manuals of publishers or scholarly societies, and studies of the English language. Many others could be added, but these in particular—some of them by chance—have been of especial use to the author of the present guide.

American Psychological Association. (1984). *Publication manual of the American Psychological Association* (3rd ed., rev.). Washington, DC: Author.

The Chicago manual of style. (1982). (13th ed.). Chicago: University of Chicago Press.

Corder, J.W., & Ruszkiewicz, J.J. (1985). *Handbook of current English* (7th ed.). Glenview, IL: Scott, Foresman.

Curme, G.O. (1947). *English grammar: The principles and practice of English grammar applied to present-day usage.* New York: Barnes & Noble.

Ebbit, W.R., & Ebbit, D.R. (1982). *Perrin's index to English* (7th ed.). Glenview, IL: Scott, Foresman.

Evans, B., & Evans, C. (1957). *A dictionary of contemporary American usage.* New York: Random House.

Follett, W. (1966). *Modern American usage: A guide.* New York: Hill & Wang.

Fowler, H.W. (1965). *A dictionary of modern English usage* (2nd ed.). Oxford: Oxford University Press, Clarendon Press.

Fowler, H.W., & Fowler, F.G. (1931). *The King's English* (3rd ed.). Oxford: Oxford University Press, Clarendon Press.

Gorrell, R., & Laird, C. (1976). *Modern English handbook* (6th ed.). Englewood Cliffs, NJ: Prentice-Hall.

Guth, H.P. (1985). *New concise handbook.* Belmont, CA: Wadsworth.

Hodges, J.C., Whitten, M.E., & Webb, S.S. (1986). *Harbrace college handbook* (10th ed.). San Diego: Harcourt Brace Jovanovich.

Huddleston, R. (1984). *Introduction to the grammar of English.* Cambridge: Cambridge University Press.

Kane, T.S. (1988). *The new Oxford guide to writing.* New York: Oxford University Press.

Morris, W., & Morris, M. (1985). *Harper dictionary of contemporary usage* (2nd ed.). New York: Harper & Row.

Quirk, R., & Greenbaum, S. (1973). *A concise grammar of contemporary English.* New York: Harcourt Brace Jovanovich.

Sternberg, R.J. (1977). *Writing the psychology paper.* Woodbury, NY: Barron's Educational Series.

Webster's dictionary of English usage. (1989). Springfield, MA: Merriam-Webster.

White, E.B. (1979). *The elements of style by William Strunk, Jr.* (3rd ed.). New York: Macmillan.

Williams, J.M. (1990). *Style: Toward clarity and grace.* Chicago: University of Chicago Press.

Willis, H. (1975). *A brief handbook of English.* New York: Harcourt Brace Jovanovich.

Words into type. (1974). (3rd ed.). Englewood Cliffs, NJ: Prentice-Hall.